New Directions for
Higher Education

Betsy Barefoot
EDITOR-IN-CHIEF

In Transition: Adult Higher Education Governance in Private Institutions

J. Richard Ellis
Stephen D. Holtrop
EDITORS

Number 159 • Fall 2012
Jossey-Bass
San Francisco

IN TRANSITION: ADULT HIGHER EDUCATION GOVERNANCE IN PRIVATE
INSTITUTIONS
J. Richard Ellis, Stephen D. Holtrop
New Directions for Higher Education, no. 159
Betsy Barefoot, Editor-in-Chief

Microfilm copies of issues and articles are available in 16mm and 35mm,
as well as microfiche in 105mm, through University Microfilms Inc., 300
North Zeeb Road, Ann Arbor, MI 48106-1346.

NEW DIRECTIONS FOR HIGHER EDUCATION (ISSN 0271-0560, electronic
ISSN 1536-0741) is part of The Jossey-Bass Higher and Adult Education
Series and is published quarterly by Wiley Subscription Services, Inc.,
A Wiley Company, at Jossey-Bass, One Montgomery Street, Suite 1200,
San Francisco, CA 94104-4594. Periodicals Postage Paid at San Fran-
cisco, California, and at additional mailing offices. POSTMASTER: Send
address changes to New Directions for Higher Education, Jossey-Bass,
One Montgomery Street, Suite 1200, San Francisco, CA 94104-4594.

New Directions for Higher Education is indexed in Current Index to Jour-
nals in Education (ERIC); Higher Education Abstracts.

SUBSCRIPTIONS cost $89 for individuals and $275 for institutions, agencies,
and libraries. See ordering information page at end of journal.

EDITORIAL CORRESPONDENCE should be sent to the Editor-in-Chief,
Betsy Barefoot, Gardner Institute, Box 72, Brevard, NC 28712.

Cover photograph © Digital Vision

www.josseybass.com

CONTENTS

EDITORS' NOTES

Just over thirty years ago, Lewis Mayhew (1980) authored the book *Surviving the Eighties: Strategies and Procedures for Solving Fiscal and Enrollment Problems* to address the commonly held expectation that American colleges and universities were about to enter an era of enrollment decline. The preface has this ominous prediction:

> The comments and advice contained herein are based on the belief that higher education in the United States, after a century of gradual and then rapid expansion, must now anticipate several decades of no growth or even decline. Some well-established institutions will adjust to this steady or declining state with only minor difficulty. But others, especially the privately controlled institutions, may experience such travail as to have their very existence seriously jeopardized. (ix)

The academic community waited for the impending crash throughout the decade, but the students kept coming. By 1988, Harrington and Summ in an article in *Academe* asked the question, "Whatever Happened to College Enrollment Crisis?" The National Center for Education Statistics (2011) records that during the 1980s and 1990s, the number of eighteen- to twenty-four-year-old students declined as predicted, but college enrollments increased. Overall, U.S. colleges and universities grew from 12 million students in 1980 to over 20 million in 2010. How did this happen? Colleges began attracting new kinds of students. In the decade from 1999 to 2009, the number of traditionally aged undergraduate students grew by only 14 percent, but total college enrollment grew by 38 percent. Adult students became a growth market, and programs designed specifically for adults became the financial saviors for many of those privately controlled institutions whose futures seemed in jeopardy in 1980.

The increase in the number of adult students and the presence of academic programs designed to meet adults' particular needs and circumstances created stress points in the administrative structures of traditional private institutions. In some cases, the programs were embraced as vital academic units that were logical extensions of the institution's historic mission. At worst, they functioned as auxiliary enterprises whose singular purpose was to generate revenue to support traditional campus operations. Whatever the goal, the programs caused institutions to modify their structures to accommodate these new students and programs.

This publication is a candid look into how some traditional liberal arts colleges have incorporated nontraditional adult degree programs. Taken together, the authors capture the emulsive nature of this imperfect blend as

NEW DIRECTIONS FOR HIGHER EDUCATION, no. 159, Fall 2012 © Wiley Periodicals, Inc.
Published online in Wiley Online Library (wileyonlinelibrary.com) • DOI:10.1002/he.20020

well as the fluidity of solutions. Regardless of how the institutions have approached this dilemma, they all share a common history of periodic change. The directions of the changes are not the same, and indeed you will note that some institutions have abandoned organizational models that others are adopting. There is no attempt here to present a unified vision of the right way to organize an institution for success. Not only does one size NOT fit all but even those universities with extensive experience in administering adult degree programs realize that their model must continue to change.

The institutional approaches to directing adult programs are categorized into three broad paradigms according to their overall governance structure: centralized, decentralized, and hybrid.

In Chapter One, Ellis begins by offering an overview of the dynamics having an impact on traditional institutions once they initiate nontraditional adult programs. The next three chapters present universities whose current structures combine the operation of adult programs within university-wide, centralized processes. In Chapter Two, Blair describes an institution that moved from a decentralized model toward a centralized structure that resulted in an increase in academic quality. Sullivan and Pagano in Chapter Three present a similar situation that involved a physical move from remote facilities back to the home campus, and in Chapter Four, Clark relates some operational frustrations with a centralized structure but acknowledges that it has led to increased buy-in from a traditional campus community.

The next two chapters represent institutions that adopted the opposite approach. Curry in Chapter Five presents the example of a private university near Chicago whose mature adult studies program takes care of its own needs, including the hiring of full-time faculty members who are independent from their traditional campus counterparts. In Chapter Six, Giles reflects on the history of adult education as well as her own experience with the adult studies program at a rural university with multicampus locations statewide and in neighboring states. She concludes that traditional institutions must be designed to respond quickly to changes in the marketplace by creating new structures focused on the needs of adult studies programs.

The next three chapters feature institutions that have developed hybrid models incorporating some aspects of centralization and decentralization. Jass in Chapter Seven describes a model in which separate administrative structures and locations are maintained but remain very connected and integrated. The model Williams presents in Chapter Eight includes outsourced services in addition to decentralized and centralized features. Finally, the model described in Chapter Nine by Cockley demonstrates healthy internal relationships and cooperation within an institution where traditional and nontraditional programs share some functions and other functions are distinct.

In Chapter Ten, Holtrop summarizes the current status of the ongoing process to incorporate nontraditional programs in traditional colleges or universities. His chapter includes data from a 2011 survey that supplements the case studies and provides a ranking of the adult program administrative functions most likely to be decentralized among the surveyed institutions.

You will note that all the authors recognize the imperfect fit of their institution's approach to addressing the oil and water of entrepreneurial programs on traditional campuses. It is hoped that their candor will make this publication a practical tool for institutions as well as a history and current picture of this under-recognized dynamic of independent colleges and universities in the United States at the beginning of the second decade of the twenty-first century.

References

Harrington, P. E., and A. M. Summ. 1988. "Whatever Happened to the College Enrollment Crisis?" *Academe* 74: 17–22.

Mayhew, L. B. 1980. *Surviving the Eighties: Strategies and Procedures for Solving Fiscal and Enrollment Problems.* San Francisco: Jossey-Bass.

National Center for Education Statistics. 2011. *Digest of Education Statistics 2010.* Washington, DC: U.S. Department of Education.

J. RICHARD ELLIS is dean of the Graduate School of John Brown University in Siloam Springs, Arkansas.

STEPHEN D. HOLTROP is dean of graduate and adult programs and professor of education at Huntington University in Huntington, Indiana.

NEW DIRECTIONS FOR HIGHER EDUCATION • DOI:10.1002/he

1

Adult degree programs have been seen as a win-win solution for private colleges and adult learners, but their innovative and often-entrepreneurial postures are not a natural fit with governance structures in more traditional institutions. Through narrative and illustrative vignettes, this chapter presents an overview of efforts employed by some institutions to strike a balance between their historic missions and these nontraditional programs.

The Win-Win of Adult Degree Programs

J. Richard Ellis

Rob was a self-described success story. In his early forties, he had a career that had given him a comfortable life in a nice home in a good community. His wife was a registered nurse; he had a daughter in college and a son in high school. His positive outlook, ever-present smile, and jovial nature made him everyone's immediate friend. Add in his competitive drive honed in high school sports and a year or two of college baseball, and it's easy to understand why he was such a successful salesman with a Fortune 500 corporation.

Then one day his boss called him in for a meeting.

"Rob, we have big plans for you, but you can't go any further without a bachelor's degree. You find a way to finish college and doors will open for you here."

Three years later, Rob was regional sales manager for his employer—with a BS degree in organizational management from an independent college in a small community.

. . . .

In some ways, the college was in an enviable position in the early 1990s. Its home campus in a small midwestern town had a record residential enrollment. Dorms were full and the classrooms and quad were buzzing with young students. But fund-raising and the endowment had not grown so fast as the enrollment, which meant that increasingly scant nontuition dollars were now being spread over more students and faculty. The campus was bumping up against capacity issues for residence halls and daytime classroom scheduling. Continued growth in the resident population would require significant brick-and-mortar investments. The college's semirural location made it attractive to prospective students and faculty, but it was beyond commuting distance for students in the larger metropolitan areas of the state.

NEW DIRECTIONS FOR HIGHER EDUCATION, no. 159, Fall 2012 © Wiley Periodicals, Inc.
Published online in Wiley Online Library (wileyonlinelibrary.com) • DOI:10.1002/he.20021

The college needed to increase the enrollment in a way that was consistent with its mission but did not require extensive capital investment in buildings. The board and president contracted with an outside agency to design a cohort-based degree completion program for working adults. Faculty, staff, and administrators created systems to recruit and serve off-campus adult students. A program director was hired, and instructional locations were established in larger population centers.

Within six years, the college had multiple locations across the state and over one thousand students enrolled in the program. Net revenue from these programs subsidized campus operations and development, at times contributing to the institution's quasi-endowment.

These accounts are two angles on the same story. The salesman who needed to finish his bachelor's degree did so at the rural college that needed to attract a commuter student population. Both stories have been repeated with minor variations at independent colleges and universities across the United States over the past quarter century. Adult degree completion programs became the win-win solution for individuals and colleges stymied by traditional assumptions in higher education.

These programs not only created a win-win solution for colleges and adult learners but also introduced a disruptive technology into the academy. Like the college in our example, many of the institutions offering adult degree completion programs were traditional liberal arts colleges with a legacy of residential education. Traditional administrative structures did not always mesh well with these innovative educational entities, which often took on an entrepreneurial posture. Some operated as auxiliary enterprises within the institutions with their own admissions staffs, academic governance, and budgetary control. Other institutions attempted to squeeze these new programs into existing organizational structures and processes.

The former approach tended to create organizational silos that became isolated from the rest of the campus; their independence gave them the flexibility to respond to changing circumstances in the marketplace but also raised questions about quality and rigor from the excluded traditional academic community. The latter approach—operating the new program from within traditional organizational structures—provided an appearance of conformity to standards and governance but may not have recognized the inherent differences in the programs and students or allowed for the administrative flexibility that characterizes successful programs for adult learners. Policies and practices designed for young, residential, first-time college students were incongruent with the needs of adult commuter students in practical terms as well as in educational philosophy.

Struggles over this organizational incongruity led inevitably to questions of institutional fit. How do adult degree completion programs fit within the mission of a residential liberal arts college? As a group, the programs have a career advancement focus that seems too vocational for some traditional institutions. The programs also tend to share common components that collide with liberal education ideals, such as a distributed general education requirement instead of a structured core curriculum, generous transfer credit policies, encouraged use of standardized tests such as the College Level Examination Program (CLEP) and DANTES Subject Standardized Tests (DSST), and the awarding of credit for noncollegiate prior learning through student-created portfolios and documentation of professional training. Degree completion programs are also typified by the use of standardized curriculum taught by adjunct faculty often drawn from industry rather than academe. And the underlying goal of net revenue generation seemed at odds with more traditional goals of higher education and a traditional financial model that subsidizes students' education through endowments and fund-raising.

Added to the concern about fit is the fact that many of the early adopters of adult degree completion programs were institutions whose mission contained a faith component. Smaller Protestant, Catholic, and interdenominational institutions saw that these cohort-based programs had the potential to generate a margin of revenue that would make a worthwhile contribution to their financial bottom lines in the short term and could have significant implications for their futures. As David Riesman (1981) noted at the time, many faith-related institutions of the late twentieth century retained a top-down administrative structure that allowed them to respond to changes in the environment at a speed unimaginable by larger, faculty-led institutions. Nonetheless, important constituencies within these colleges and universities saw potential conflicts between the historic religious mission of the institutions and this new educational enterprise.

Invoking Faustian imagery, faculty and others cautioned that the institutions were endangering their "missional souls" for the sake of financial futures. How could these adjunct faculty members be expected to integrate faith and learning or communicate the mission values of the institution to commuting adult students, many of whom would never set foot on the home campus? How can such institutions fulfill their historic mission through this nontraditional methodology? How do we safeguard our legacy?

The organizational approaches traditional institutions adopted to incorporate nontraditional programs for adults into their administrative structures can be placed in three categories: centralized, distributed, and hybrid governance models. With **centralized** models, institutions use campuswide offices and administrative structures for all programs, both the traditional and nontraditional. Examples would include one registrar's office, one dean, one marketing and enrollment office, one academic unit per discipline, and so forth, serving the entire institution.

Institutions with **distributed** models of adult education decentralize these functions into distinct entities for the traditional program and the nontraditional program(s). Such institutions might have a registrar for traditional programs and another registrar or at least a separate assistant registrar for nontraditional programs, a traditional business division and a separate academic unit overseeing nontraditional business programs, separate academic governance structures for traditional and nontraditional programs, and a marketing and recruiting office focusing on high school seniors and another on adult learners. Although recognizing that no institution has perfectly centralized or completely distributed its adult degree program functions, those following a **hybrid** model intentionally incorporate a mix of centralized and distributed governance structures.

Centralized Governance

The right decision about how to incorporate the adult studies program was obvious to the provost. There was no need to create separate support and academic structures. He had heard horror stories from colleagues at other institutions about renegade degree completion departments; he was not going to allow that to happen here. No systems are perfect, but the current governance and support processes that had evolved over decades worked fine for the rest of the campus, and there was no reason to predict they would not work for this new initiative as well.

The modern postsecondary institution has all the complexities of a city or corporation and nearly as many constituents to satisfy. From recruitment through alumni relations and all steps in between, a college or university has a multifaceted and evolving relationship with its students. Consider financial aid with all its federal requirements, student accounts, athletics, student life, library and other learning support entities, the registrar's office, student support services, the bookstore, food service . . . and that's only a fraction of the enterprise. There are physical assets such as buildings and technology infrastructure to maintain. Financial operations need to run in an efficient and accountable manner. Advancement and public relations guard and attempt to mold the institution's public brand. The institution is accountable to external entities including accrediting agencies and state and federal governments. Internally, there is that dynamic unique to higher education—faculty governance—and its complex relationship to curriculum approval, course design, professional evaluation and promotion, and assessment of student learning. Each area requires personnel with specific knowledge, background, and expertise.

In their history of American higher education, Cohen and Kisker (2009) begin by noting that "practically every aspect" of contemporary colleges and universities can be traced back to the nineteenth century, the Colonial Era, or even medieval Europe (1). At individual institutions, systems and traditions emerge to define the relationships between constituencies and structures. As was described previously, nontraditional innovations such as adult degree completion programs tend to disrupt the institutional equilibrium, and colleges use various approaches to address the disruption.

Institutions with a centralized governance structure for the adult studies programs embrace the concept that each functional area should serve the entire institution, including the adult degree programs. The goal is to achieve synergies rather than duplication of effort. This model also maintains academic and budgetary control of the adult studies programs within the normal institution-wide offices. The concept appears to make sense intuitively. Why create two financial aid offices or admissions offices? Shouldn't the same academic unit responsible for traditional undergraduate business degree programs also oversee the business degree completion program for adult learners? This model tends to deemphasize the entrepreneurial nature of adult degree programs and focus on the commonalities of all academic enterprises within the institution.

Distributed Authority

According to the dean of the adult studies programs, the key to their success has been the ability to respond quickly to opportunities as they present themselves. This was possible only because her program was not bound to timeworn structures of the traditional campus-bound processes. The undergraduate admissions office that was so successful in attracting high school seniors nationally was clueless about how to market to working adults in its own metropolitan area. Rules and policies designed for residential first-time college students would place unnecessary restrictions on transfer students with two or three years of college credit, years of employer-based training, and credit for military service. The conventional governance and committee structures took months—if not years—to approve even the smallest changes in policies. By being allowed to create their own academic policies, run their own admissions office, attract and train adjunct faculty from outside the academy and pay them on a different pay scale, the degree completion program staff members had graduated hundreds of adult students and generated significant net revenue for the institution. Without this structure, the inertia of university traditions and protocols would have turned their innovative enterprise into just another night school. She was convinced of this.

Ask an adult educator to describe a successful program for adult learners and somewhere in the description will appear the words "innovative" and "entrepreneurial." Lee Bash (2003) has noted that many universities recognize a large potential market of adult students, but they may not be prepared for the changes necessary to serve those adult learners well. In many cases, these programs are designed expressly for individuals who were not served by traditional higher education offerings and are looking for something designed to serve them now (Wlodkowski 2008). Adult educators want to implement curriculum and instructional methodologies developed specifically for adults (Knowles, Holton, and Swanson 2005). To the true believer, the education of adults is more than just a new revenue stream for their institution; it is a way to change the world (Brookfield and Holst 2010).

The dean in the example represents the type of institution that responded to the need for innovation in adult educational programs by developing processes and structures that are largely independent of the traditional campus organizational architecture. This approach provides maximum flexibility to respond quickly to changes in the marketplace. It allows adult education administrators to be certain that their students' needs and circumstances are at the forefront of policy decisions. It is not surprising that many of the larger adult studies programs are managed with a high level of autonomy.

And yet when does the adult program become autonomous to the point of no longer representing the host institution? What prevents administrative flexibility from disconnecting the entrepreneurial adult studies program from the historic institution whose name and identity it shares? External constituents may not view the various units of the college or university with a level of specificity that distinguishes between the nontraditional and the traditional elements. Internal constituents, however, can be intensely aware that the adult studies program operates outside the normal structures and restrictions that regulate the rest of the campus. In such cases, the adult program administrator may feel somewhat marginalized within the institution (Watkins and Tisdell 2006).

Hybrid Models of Governance

Richard Alfred noted in 2006 that American higher education was entering a "volatile new era of competition in which the deftness of an institution's strategy will have a lot to do with its success" (188). He admonished college and university leaders to see the big picture and recognize the need to adapt to changing conditions, roles, and relationships that characterize the environments in which postsecondary institutions operate at the beginning of the twenty-first century. This need for deft strategy applies to our discussion of how traditional liberal arts colleges and universities can best serve adult learners and incorporate the administration of those programs into their governance structures.

Advocates of hybrid models of governance attempt to avoid the "hobgoblin of consistency" by not being held captive by either exclusive model. They adopt elements of the decentralized model that allow for greater flexibility in responding to changeable markets and the needs and expectations of adult learners. Simultaneously, they maintain centralization in areas that lead to greater efficiencies of effort or ensure more appropriate academic oversight of teaching and learning. In some cases, hybridization emerges as a result of a series of marginal changes; for example, a university with a centralized structure for its adult studies programs decides to create an independent student recruitment staff and office, or a decentralized institution determines that a single financial aid office allows individual staff members to develop expertise in the peculiarities of specific Title IV programs that are used by both traditional and nontraditional students. Over time, the centralized or decentralized model loses its consistency as it becomes more of a pragmatic amalgam. In other cases, there is intentionality from the outset to incorporate elements of each approach into a unique structure that works best within the institution's culture and mission.

The appeal of this approach is obvious. By taking the best of both worlds, it would appear that the college or university has the flexibility to change as circumstances require or whenever the model seems to be failing in a particular area. For example, an institution decided to abandon the decentralized admissions functions by centralizing all student recruitment efforts under one university admissions department. Traditional undergraduate, graduate, and adult degree completion recruiting moved from independent offices to one unified office reporting to the vice president for enrollment. But when the expected synergies of having one department coordinating the promotion of all the programs of the institution did not materialize after a number of years, the university returned to a decentralized model, first for graduate admissions and then for adult degree completion recruiting. The hybrid approach to governance allows this ebb and flow of centralization and decentralization of particular areas of the adult education initiative without requiring a major restructuring of the whole.

It could be argued that a centralized-decentralized hybrid model represents a more natural model for the institution and the adult studies unit. A decentralized model implies that an adult studies program is so different from the rest of the institution that it cannot survive within the larger institutional structure. It assumes that the larger college or university culture and structure represent a harmful environment for adult programs. Centralization, on the other hand, could be interpreted as overly controlling, communicating a lack of trust in those administrators in charge of the adult programs. It has the potential of dismissing the legitimate differences between adult learners and traditional undergraduates and thereby severely limiting the adult program's potential.

A hybrid model attempts to recognize the differences and the similarities between the management of adult studies programs and the rest of the institution. It requires those involved with adult programs to be part of the larger institution while advocating for their particular areas of concern. "Like other university administrators, adult degree program administrators must constantly scan the horizon and negotiate power and interest" (Watkins and Tisdell 2006, 141). The burden lies with the adult educators to "move institutional interest in adult degree programs from more marginal positions closer to the center" (153).

No Single Solution

The best fit for adult studies program within the structures of traditional colleges and universities depends on the institutions. As the other chapters in this publication illustrate, there are success stories as well as failures connected to centralized, decentralized, and hybrid models. The importance of the unique organizational dynamics of each institution cannot be overemphasized. Is the institution open to innovation? Is there sufficient unused capacity within existing systems to accommodate the addition of new programs and students? Are structures (and people) adaptable to change? Do offices and departments see the bigger picture with reference to their larger constituencies, or are they so focused on their traditional populations that they see the new students as someone else's concern? How does an adult studies program stay connected to a traditional liberal arts institution while maintaining the flexibility to adapt to changes in the marketplace and keep up with the consumerist needs of adult learners?

Staying connected to the institution without being tied down by the timeworn bureaucracies that can characterize traditional colleges is a concept Gordon MacKenzie (1998) cleverly describes as "orbiting the giant hairball." In MacKenzie's imagery, the "hairball" represents an organization's bramble of rules, policies, procedures, traditions, and other operational dynamics that are based on past needs. Consequently, they can ensnare creative innovation. Enterprises such as adult studies programs need to stay connected to the host institution without being entangled in processes and protocols that were not designed with the new endeavor in mind. Whatever approaches a college or university takes to structuring adult studies programs, the successful institution will acknowledge the specific needs of adult learners and will design processes that are able to serve this growing segment of higher education. The result can be a win-win that provides needed educational services to adults and an expanded mission for the institution.

References

Alfred, R. L. 2006. *Managing the Big Picture in Colleges and Universities: From Tactics to Strategies*. Westport, CT: American Council on Education/Praeger.

Bash, L. 2003. *Adult Learners in the Academy*. Bolton, MA: Anker.

Brookfield, S. D., and J. D. Holst. 2010. *Radicalizing Learning: Adult Education for a Just World*. San Francisco: Jossey-Bass.

Cohen, A. M., and C. B. Kisker. 2009. *The Shaping of American Higher Education: Emergence and Growth of the Contemporary System*, 2nd ed. San Francisco: Jossey-Bass.

Knowles, M. S., E. F. Holton, and R. A. Swanson. 2005. *The Adult Learner*, 6th ed. Burlington, MA: Elsevier Butterworth Heinemann.

MacKenzie, G. 1998. *Orbiting the Giant Hairball: A Corporate Fool's Guide to Surviving with Grace*. New York: Viking.

Riesman, D. 1981. "Evangelical Colleges: Untouched by the Academic Revolution." *Change* 13(1): 13–20.

Watkins, B. J., and E. J. Tisdell. 2006. "Negotiating the Labyrinth from Margin to Center: Adult Degree Program Administrators as Program Planners Within Higher Education Institutions." *Adult Education Quarterly* 56: 134–159.

Wlodkowski, R. J. 2008. *Enhancing Adult Motivation to Learn: A Comprehensive Guide for Teaching All Adults*, 3rd ed. San Francisco: Jossey-Bass.

J. Richard Ellis *is dean of the Graduate School of John Brown University in Siloam Springs, Arkansas. He established the university's multisite adult degree completion program and directed it from 1993 to 2010.*

2

Eastern University has moved from a distributed model to a centralized model for administration of its adult degree programs. Although the move was undertaken to address perceived inefficiencies in student services, which have not been entirely remedied, an unintended benefit of the restructuring was improvement of academic quality.

Mission Intentionality and Operational Integrity: The Essential Role of Faculty in Adult Degree Programs

Anthony L. Blair

Between 2003 and 2006, Eastern University, a pioneer and significant player in adult education in the Delaware and Susquehanna Valleys of Pennsylvania, accomplished a challenging and awkward transition from a distributed administrative model for its adult degree programs to a more centralized approach. This transition involved numerous factors and motivations but one central component in the ultimate success of that transition was a significant change in the role of faculty assigned to the program. Once regarded as rather ancillary providers of instructional services, reporting to nonacademic administrators, they were increasingly empowered to assume ownership of three primary inputs of academic quality: curriculum, instruction, and admission of students. The drivers of this change, the process that was followed, and the consequences that resulted are briefly discussed in this chapter, allowing the reader to generalize from Eastern University's experience to other institutions exploring or desiring such a transition.

In 2003, the nontraditional adult programs of the university were housed either in the School of Professional Studies (SPS) or the School of International Leadership and Development (SILD). Although together they offered both undergraduate and graduate programs, both of these schools were distinct in identity and administered separately (and differently) from the traditional undergraduate School of Arts and Sciences and the traditional graduate school (known as the School for Social Change). In fact, both schools were so distinct and separate from the traditional programs as to be located off the main campus. SPS rented space in the American Baptist headquarters some five miles from the St. Davids, Pennsylvania, campus. SILD occupied rental space at the National Christian Conference Center five miles

New Directions for Higher Education, no. 159, Fall 2012 © Wiley Periodicals, Inc.
Published online in Wiley Online Library (wileyonlinelibrary.com) • DOI:10.1002/he.20022

farther west. Both used classrooms on campus, but the majority of their instruction took place in churches, corporate boardrooms, and classrooms at other academic institutions with which they had partnered. Some of these were located internationally, in Asia and Africa in particular.

The programs they offered included undergraduate degree completion programs in organizational management, management of information systems, and nursing, as well as graduate degrees in management, health administration, nonprofit management, organizational leadership, and international development. Most of the latter were master's in business administration (MBA) programs. The instruction was offered primarily by adjunct practitioner faculty, supplemented occasionally by full-time faculty borrowed from other departments. SILD had no resident faculty of its own; its staff of six was composed solely of administrators and staff. SPS had seven resident faculty members who, however, had no instructional responsibilities in their standard workload (although most supplemented their salaries by taking overload responsibilities as adjunct instructors in their own programs). These seven had been hired originally as research advisers and academic advisers. Despite their being granted faculty status by action of the university faculty and the board of trustees in 2000, their responsibilities or decision-making authority had not changed. In 2003, the faculty of SPS had little to no input on any of the three primary factors that determine instructional quality: instruction, curriculum, and admission of students. As a result of this marginalization of faculty members within these nontraditional adult programs, the academic quality of the programs and, indeed, the academic reputation of the nontraditional faculty were both regarded as suspect by most of the rest of the university faculty.

By 2006, things had changed dramatically. A structural realignment of the university had created the Campolo College of Graduate and Professional Studies (CCGPS), which was a merger of SPS, SILD, and the School for Social Change. This merged college served only adult students, and its student population (2,000) was roughly equal to that of the traditional undergraduate college. Within CCGPS, academic programs had been redistributed among units, and unit names had been changed (the former SPS and SILD emerged as the School of Management Studies and the School of Leadership and Development, respectively) but the most significant internal change was that each unit was now regarded as a fully functioning academic department, on par with traditional academic departments, each with its own faculty, chair, and responsibility for academic quality. Within a year of the merger, the Campolo College had moved to the main campus and was housed in a new administrative and classroom building created specifically for its use.

A primary motive for the merger of the units serving adult populations was the opportunity to achieve greater efficiencies in the support services of these units. Prior to the merger, each unit had been forced to create its own administrative structures and processes, including marketing and recruitment, admissions, registrar, curricular materials delivery, contracts,

instructional contracts, payroll, accounting, student services, distance learning support, and facilities management. Although some of these functions
were theoretically linked or supervised by their parallel structures on the
main campus, they were, for all intents and purposes, redundant. The redun-
dancy was needed, it had been argued, in order to meet the unique needs of
students in alternative delivery methods. With the merger of the units, those
separate functions were mostly brought together under a single administrative structure, and some were even merged with the centralized functions
that primarily served traditional students.

Creating efficiencies from the merger was more difficult than anticipated, however, as CCGPS provided instruction in a bewildering array of
instructional levels (noncredit, associate's, bachelor's, master's, and doctoral
levels); delivery models (accelerated deliveries as well as traditional programs for graduate students); locations (more than two dozen classroom
sites domestically and more internationally); distance options (some entirely
online, some with a residency–online hybrid, some on-ground with
an online supplement, and some entirely on-ground); and calendars (some
year-round with five-, six-, or eight-week terms and others semester based
with summers off). It was difficult to train and equip CCGPS personnel to
provide contextualized support services across such a spectrum at the same
level of quality that had previously been provided by smaller units when
each had to care for only one or two specific delivery models or variables.

Five years later, many of the administrative challenges of the merger
remain. Some of the academic departments have once again created redundant structures and hired additional administrative personnel in order to better serve students and adjunct instructors whom they believe were less well
supported with the merged services. Additionally, despite stated intentions
to merge more unique CCGPS administrative services with those of the traditional programs, few of these mergers have actually occurred. Those that
are required by law or deemed essential for university integrity, such as financial aid and student accounts, have frequently (and perhaps unfairly) been
viewed by faculty and administrators of the adult degree programs as being
insufficiently sensitive to or supportive of the unique needs of adult students.

It may be argued, then, that the original motivation for the merger of
the programs serving adult students has not yet been achieved, and it is
entirely possible that it may never be achieved. There has, however, been
another implication of the merger, and one that may have more significant
long-term benefits to the adult degree programs than any perceived or
desired efficiency of support services. That implication is the improved academic quality, in both perception and reality, of most of the degree programs
offered to adult students. That improvement in academic quality was due
largely to pressures created by the merger to create fully functioning academic departments, each with its own faculty that would have roles and
authorities comparable to those of faculty elsewhere in the university. This
transition took place through several distinct phases.

NEW DIRECTIONS FOR HIGHER EDUCATION • DOI:10.1002/he

First, the adult departments were populated with credentialed faculty. The School of Leadership and Development, which had no resident faculty at the beginning of this era and was led by a nonacademic assistant dean, created a new faculty position each year for a period of five years. This school now houses five resident faculty members, one of whom serves as the chair. The School of Management Studies (SMS), which had resident faculty members who were without standard faculty roles and responsibilities, altered the duties of those faculty members from primary service as full-time research advisors and academic advisors to instruction, research, and curriculum writing; additional nonfaculty academic advisors were hired to support their work. These faculty members can now seek tenure and promotion within the university system without the previous impediments to such, because they have functions that largely parallel those of their peers.

Second, the faculty of these programs gained oversight of the curriculum of their programs. Both units used primarily modularized curricula, which consisted of a master syllabus and fully developed lesson plans that guaranteed some level of consistency from one classroom to another, as most of the courses were taught by practitioners without instructional design experience (and sometimes without theoretical foundations). This modularized curriculum, however, had been created through contracts with content experts chosen by nonacademic administrators and had been reviewed primarily by those same nonacademic administrators. There had been few quality control mechanisms in place to guarantee the quality and appropriateness of the curriculum distributed to students and adjunct faculty. Once the full-time faculty gained control of the curricular processes, program learning goals were more closely aligned with course objectives, and course objectives were more closely aligned with learning activities. Full-time instructional designers were hired in both departments to work alongside faculty and outside content experts to provide professional expertise on such matters. Program faculty and instructional designers made sweeping changes including adding, deleting, or modifying courses; discontinuing programs; adding new program alternatives; and implementing assessment processes. For the most part, these programs are judged by students, peers, and external accreditors as possessing greater credibility and academic rigor.

Third, a similar process occurred in regard to instructional quality when the full-time faculty gained oversight of the recruitment, scheduling, training, and evaluation of adjunct instructors in their programs. These functions had all been previously performed by nonacademic administrators, with the result that those with a reputation for strong teaching and facilitation skills were far too often assigned to courses for which they lacked academic or even practitioner credentials. There were no clear criteria for the assignment or scheduling of instructors and, as there was a financial incentive in such assignments, the process was perceived as overly political.

Upon gaining oversight of these functions, the SMS faculty reviewed the credentials and teaching evaluations of all of its 300 or so adjunct instructors and certified them for specific courses in specific programs. This resulted in the dismissal of some instructors and the voluntary departure of others; some found themselves teaching fewer courses more often, some were given fewer courses overall, and others were offered additional assignments due to previously unnoticed qualifications and strengths. The faculty also planned their own training events for these adjuncts, attempting to model in the training the same andragogical principles the instructors were expected to practice in the classroom. In the aggregate, instructional quality improved noticeably.

Fourth, the faculty sought and gained greater input into admissions decisions, because one primary concern instructors expressed was the apparent lack of academic preparation of some of the students in these degree programs. Admissions criteria had been earlier approved by the university's curriculum and policy committee, a faculty function, but exceptions to admissions policy by nonacademic administrators had become so common as to effectively nullify those criteria. There were, of course, significant financial incentives and pressures from the recruitment staff to admit unprepared students, in addition to the more positive motive of providing access to transformative higher education to underserved populations, which was and remains an institutional commitment. Instructors found themselves unable to teach at a level appropriate for the course or the program when a significant percentage of the students were not equipped to follow or perform at that level, and this had the usual effects on both academic quality and grade inflation.

When one of the SMS faculty members was promoted to an administrative position (the first administrator with academic credentials and appreciation for the faculty role), the department chairs and program directors were given the opportunity for input into all requests for exceptions to admission policies. From that point forward, all admitted students met the admissions policy established by the faculty through their policy committees or were recommended to the dean for an exception to policy by the chair and program director of the department in which they would study. Faculty thus took responsibility for deciding whom they would and could teach in their own programs.

These four significant changes—the creation of fully functioning academic departments with their own resident faculty, the granting of curricular oversight to the faculty of those departments, the granting of instructional oversight to those same faculty, and the strengthening of admissions decisions with the input of those faculty—together served to improve the reputation of the adult degree programs, as well as the perception (derived from informal student feedback) of improved quality of the learning experience of those adult students. These changes were a direct result of the university's decision to move from a distributive administrative model to a more centralized model for those programs, although, ironically, the original motive for that centralization—greater efficiency of support services for the adult programs—has not been fully realized. The unintended benefit, however, has been worth the costs and headaches of that centralization, not only for the faculty and the students in those programs but also for the university in its commitment to provide transformative higher education to adult students in a faith-based learning environment.

Other institutions attempting a transition from a distributive to a centralized administrative model may profit from Eastern's experience by doing the following:

(1) Realistically estimating the administrative efficiencies gained from such centralization, even if the number and complexity of the adult programs is significantly less than that of Eastern University;

(2) Recognizing that academic quality is largely predicated upon faculty oversight of curriculum, instruction, and admissions—the three primary inputs into the student's learning experience;

(3) Providing opportunities for faculty members to function in roles that are parallel to those of faculty elsewhere in the institution, with concomitant opportunities for tenure, promotion, research, and service in greater college or university functions;

(4) Creating or modifying support services and assessment processes that fully comprehend the unique needs of adult students and the unique program deliveries that are created to serve them; and

(5) Appointing to administrative oversight of such programs only those who are both familiar with the dynamics of adult degree programs and are appreciative of the benefits provided by an expert and qualified corps of faculty

Perhaps the most important consideration to be drawn from this experience is the one assumed but not yet stated in this chapter—that institutions of higher education should view their adult learning programs as uniquely vibrant expressions of their mission, rather than as funding mechanisms for traditional programs or, worse, as a distraction from their core mission. Those who embrace adult higher education as mission fulfillment will be far more committed than others to doing so in a manner that communicates intentionality and operationalizes integrity.

ANTHONY L. BLAIR *is president of Evangelical Theological Seminary in Myerstown, Pennsylvania. Previously, he was dean of the Campolo College of Graduate and Professional Studies of Eastern University in St. Davids, Pennsylvania.*

Eastern University enrolls 4,000 students. The nontraditional programs, first launched in 1988, enroll 1,000 students and include undergraduate and graduate degrees in business, education, and nursing.

NEW DIRECTIONS FOR HIGHER EDUCATION • DOI:10.1002/he

3

In ten years, Alaska Pacific University has moved from a totally decentralized administration of its adult online program to a very centralized structure. Drastic changes in funding sources and student needs have compelled the university to take new approaches. As the learning landscape continues to shift for adults, online learners, and Alaska Native communities, the university continues to adapt its organizational structures to best address the shifting environment.

Relevant Adult Programs, Resilient Students, and Retention-Driven Administration

Esther Beth Sullivan, Rosanne V. Pagano

Alaska Pacific University (APU) is a private liberal arts university that upholds its faith-based heritage in part by meeting the needs of Alaska Native adults seeking higher education for professional and personal enrichment. APU's Rural Alaska Native Adult Distance Education Program (RANA) was initiated in the late 1990s to provide educational access to Alaska's remote and often roadless communities. Begun as a discrete, stand-alone unit, RANA has since evolved, with academic and programmatic responsibilities centralized within the institution's administrative operations.

As a case study of how an adult program develops administratively, analysis of the RANA Program within APU's structure suggests that centralized administrative structures can enhance institution-wide support for adult learning and programmatic sustainability. By aligning the adult program with the institution's liberal arts mission and supporting the program through institution-wide services, RANA moved from APU's periphery to its core. Correlated with this shift, the program saw increased rates of retention. On the other hand, diminishing program-specific identification and services—and the related dynamic of casting the adult Alaska Native student as similar to any other traditional student—posed the risk of alienation and disaffection rather that affiliation and persistence. As such, administrative staff championed the development of discrete, programmatic identity within, but distinct from, traditional liberal arts programs as instrumental to institutional affiliation and subsequent retention. In retrospect, the more that retention strategies particular to adult students were stressed across the spectrum of administrative operations, the more effective the centralized

NEW DIRECTIONS FOR HIGHER EDUCATION, no. 159, Fall 2012 © Wiley Periodicals, Inc.
Published online in Wiley Online Library (wileyonlinelibrary.com) • DOI:10.1002/he.20023

model was judged to be by all stakeholders, including students, faculty, staff, trustees, and benefactors.

This chapter describes APU's efforts to transition a distinct academic program from distributed to centralized administration, without losing the program's distinctiveness. Attention to foundational values of resilience, service, and leadership proved essential. These core values, embraced in the university mission, and most compelling in relation to the aspirations of our adult Alaska Native students, became the common thematic ground upon which centralized administration could develop—to the benefit of a once distributed program.

The Institution, the Program, Its Centralized Structure

Alaska Pacific University is a relatively new institution—chartered in 1959, the same year Alaska achieved statehood. The university's birth and endurance can be attributed in part to its original mission. Peter Gordon Gould, born in 1901 on the island of Unga in the Aleutian chain, became the first Alaska Native to be ordained as a Methodist minister and was later recognized as the founder of the university. He was noted for his tireless fund-raising efforts on behalf of the new college. His aspiration for the school was to train "Alaskans to be tomorrow's leaders—in Alaska" (Hayden 2008, 12). From its inception to the present, key themes have remained consistent in the university's mission: Christian heritage; the provision of liberal education through vital experience, later described as active learning; development of leadership, particularly in and for Alaska; and celebration of diversity and pluralism, later expanded to welcoming of learners of all ages with a special commitment to Alaska Natives (Hayden 2008).

As a private liberal arts institution situated in a state with a population of fewer than a million residents, APU's defining attribute has also been its most significant challenge. The school has always been small and student centered by design. However, on two occasions in its history, the school has been on the verge of collapse due to low enrollments. Across the most recent decade, enrollments have stabilized, hovering around 550 FTE, resulting in strategic plans that predict sustainability with slight growth. Consequently, while maintaining its tradition of undergraduate study grounded in the liberal arts, the institution has also been necessarily adaptive, embracing more specifically targeted, professionally oriented programs in order to grow enrollments. As an example, in the late 1980s, the university established a degree completion program with evening courses offered in an intensive module format. This initiative expanded APU's educational profile to serve working adults pursuing degrees in organizational administration. By the late 1990s, as this program grew to comprise approximately 10 percent of total FTE, APU was poised to develop yet another pathway for adult learners. At that point, RANA was initiated as a low residency, distance education program. It was designed to provide educational access for rural Alaskan communities, taking full advantage of the online systems that were just beginning to provide new levels of connectivity across the state.

The RANA Program was born as a small program inside a small university, grounded in Gould's founding mission of training leaders from Alaska in Alaska. As originally envisioned, the program offered areas of study to meet the professional needs of rural Alaskan communities. In such communities, professional transience still remains a crippling condition. With few homegrown, organizational administrators and credentialed teachers, rural communities are constantly recruiting outsiders to cover these crucial professional positions. Unfortunately, for a variety of reasons, there is a high turnover rate among such recruits. The toll on small communities is great, given that each recruit represents significant time and effort taken away from fundamental undertakings such as subsistence and community sustainability. Experiencing this dynamic, all of Alaska's institutions of higher education have developed educational outreach efforts aimed at developing professionals from within Alaska. In concert with those efforts, APU devised the RANA Program, enabling the rural adult learner to earn a degree while living and working in his or her home community. Baccalaureate degrees would be offered online and majors were developed to address the specific professional needs of rural Alaska: education, organizational management, and health services administration.

From inception, RANA's programmatic structure featured a brief, on-campus residency followed by online learning activities. This structure was embraced as a way to offer adult students a delivery option that was not dependent upon geographic location and that would take into consideration time-bound constraints related to work, family, and community responsibilities. As part of the program, a required, face-to-face residency at the start of each semester (three to four days on APU's campus) was instituted. The residency was designed to provide an intensive opportunity for students to meet instructors, advisors, and fellow students; receive necessary technology training and other skills development; and bond in a community of learners. Following the residency, all other activities were to occur online. Another programmatic feature included the scheduling of synchronous chat sessions once a week for each course. Other class activities—such as discussion, collaboration, writing, and assessment—were to be facilitated asynchronously through online systems. Given this programmatic structure—involving all the usual aspects of educational operations, but compounded by other distinctive tasks ranging from travel-related assistance to management of sophisticated technology systems—dedicated administrative oversight developed in order to coordinate the multiple physical, technological, educational, human, and financial resources necessary to support the program's structure.

Not surprisingly, given its particular mission and its distinctive programmatic features, RANA was conceived of as a decentralized, discrete unit in relation to the institution's centralized administrative structure. The opportunity to develop this kind of distributed unit within the financially constrained environment of APU arose from the availability of external funding. A significant seed grant was awarded to the school in 1999 from the Rasmuson Foundation, one of the few family-based foundations in Alaska. The foundation's purpose is to invest "both in individuals and well-managed 501(c)(3) organizations dedicated to improving the quality of life for Alaskans" (http://www.rasmuson.org). Complementary missions led the foundation to fund the build-up of APU's technology infrastructure so the university could initiate distance education offerings. In 2000, on the heels of the Rasmuson award, the university received a sizable three-year grant from the U.S. Department of Education to add a teacher education major to the RANA Program.

By 2004, the RANA Program had developed in a distributed fashion with its own program director, associate director, and admissions counselor, as well as technologists and instructors. In addition to providing clear administrative lines of oversight for a complex educational operation, distributed administration included a self-contained cost unit that could receive external funding. Across the first five years of operation, nearly 100 percent of RANA's direct operational expenses (as well as significant levels of indirect costs) was covered by external funding. In the pursuit of such sponsorship and with need for discrete financial accountability, distributed administration was a definite advantage to the program.

The Context, the Challenge, the Transition to Centralized Administration

The RANA Program developed in an environment where external sponsorship for such initiatives was plentiful. 2004 marked another year in which the program received significant grants from the federal government, with awards totaling nearly $2 million. Nevertheless, in that same year, federal program directors and representatives made it clear that the funding context from which these awards had arisen was changing dramatically. Even with multiyear grants rolling into the university to support the RANA Program, APU had to begin planning for the program's sustainability without the kind of subsidies that had led to its creation.

At a glance, the five-year-old RANA Program of 2004 looked progressive in mission and design but challenged by the most basic problem for small institutions: low enrollment. In the fall of that year, with 20 FTE, RANA comprised less than 3 percent of APU's total FTE. Even more pressing, enrollments for online courses were not meeting the minimum number of participants to warrant offerings. At that level, the program was not viable. It was particularly unsustainable given its decentralized administration and labor-intensive structure. In spite of this condition, the institution maintained a strong commitment to supporting and developing the program. This commitment was evidenced in the university's strategic planning documents of 2004 and 2006, where increasing the numbers of RANA students and online offerings was listed as a key goal. Dedicated to the mission and design of the program, APU began reevaluating the program's administrative structure with an eye toward changes that could be financially sustained and would produce operations to recruit and retain more students. The process of evaluation took place throughout APU's governing and administrative culture, involving the president's council and faculty and staff committees.

The resulting transition was a move from a distributed to centralized administrative structure. Centralization of administration occurred as student-related operations were transferred from the discrete oversight of RANA staff to university-wide systems, departments, and offices. Where RANA students had originally been advised by RANA advisors, the transition moved toward assigning advisors from the ranks of regular faculty. Where online courses had routinely been taught by adjunct instructors hired and trained by RANA staff, the transition moved toward academic departments assigning online courses just as any other courses might be assigned to regular faculty workloads. And, where student financial aid and registration had once been channeled through RANA communications, the transition moved toward connecting students with the central university offices for such services.

However, while RANA was generally moving toward more integration with the central university structures, distance education programs created new challenges. The changing nature of higher education in the twenty-first century—with the reach for the first time of for-profit institutions into Alaska—necessitated a different institutional approach to distance education. The university as a whole needed to move toward an embrace, if not a full realization, of online offerings and online accessibility. Departments and offices that had not had responsibilities in relation to the university's online presence needed to become part of APU's distance education efforts. To meet this challenge, the position of RANA director was recast as the director of distance education, with university-wide administrative oversight of distance education operations and offerings, including, but not exclusive to, the RANA Program.

The Students, the Plans, the Outcomes

The story of RANA's changing administrative structure cannot be separated from the students the program was designed to serve. Originally offered as outreach to rural Alaskan communities, where 80 percent of the population is of Alaska Native heritage, RANA was designed to serve rural Alaska Native adults. On the other hand, the program was always open to non-Native participants as well. Although all of the initial fifteen participants were Alaska Native, in the transitional year of 2004 with twice as many participants, 73 percent of participants were Alaska Native. Similarly, although the program initially targeted rural communities, participants increasingly came from all across the state. In its first year, all of the RANA participants came from communities off the road system in Alaska. However, by 2004, 21 percent of participants were living in the Anchorage area. With a modest level of diversification of student population, the 2004–05 academic year then marked a point at which the university grappled not just with administrative models, but also with mission and growth. How could the program become better positioned to connect with a growing demand for online offerings irrespective of geographic or cultural emphasis? More important, how could the program expand its offerings and outreach without losing sight of its founding mission?

With the need to increase enrollments and offerings and with an administrative structure making the transition from distributed to centralized oversight, 2005–06 became another crucial year in RANA's history. At that point, the institution developed two major goals for the program: address recruitment and focus on retention.

The recruitment plan for RANA prioritized two coordinated undertakings: expansion of recruitment territories and program branding. Previous to this plan, funding for RANA had always supported program-specific staff appointments. Moving in a new direction, the plan focused on coordinating the previously decentralized operations with the more centralized ones of the university's admissions office. In particular, admissions would take the lead in developing a campaign to expand RANA's identification with roadless communities to include and recruit from communities on the road system and by extension from within the Anchorage area where nearly half of the state's population resides. Recruitment efforts expanded to involve more RANA promotion at events and forums within a fifty-mile radius of Anchorage, advertising placements on radio stations with markets located on the highway, and statewide direct mailings to include both Alaska Native–serving organizations and other lists of professional offices with interests related to RANA's current offerings.

Feeding into this campaign was a branding effort that positioned RANA first and foremost as an Alaska-based distance education program, committed to growing leadership from within Alaska. The central premise was that by serving the professional and educational needs of rural Alaska, the program could serve the needs of working adults from all across the state. Visually, the branding effort put the faces of RANA front and center. APU students of Alaska Native descent were featured, and images that resonated with Alaska Native culture were used to develop visual emphasis. All textual information included phrases emphasizing the pressing professional needs of rural Alaska. Thematically, the branding initiative stressed appreciation for the abiding resilience of Alaska communities and working adults pursuing education; the existent and emerging leadership within Alaska that could be fostered to meet professional needs particularly within the education, profit, and nonprofit sectors of the state; and the deep understandings that arise where research is informed by local knowledge and vice versa.

RANA's recruitment plan established admissions targets and developed outreach and branding strategies to realize those targets. Similarly, the retention plan established retention targets and laid out strategies. Even more than the recruitment plan, RANA's retention plan reflected a centralized approach in which oversight, responsibilities, and accountability were shared among the various offices and departments in the institution. The plan focused specifically on setting, documenting, and improving semester-to-semester retention rates. From registration and financial aid, to delivery of online courses and services, to communication streams and community building, nearly every operation of the institution was referenced. In particular, three strategies required a centralized approach: development of a two-year scheduling matrix so that students could plan ahead for offerings; development of online interfaces for registration and financial aid; and development of ongoing communication streams to keep students connected to course, program, and university information. Previous RANA directors had been responsible for a decentralized program and accountable in significant ways to external sponsors. Given the framework of the retention plan, the newly appointed director of distance education was more directly accountable to the academic administration of the university and responsible for coordinating institution-wide operations along with other directors, department chairpersons, and administrators in order to realize the goals of the plan. As such, the director was included as a member on significant oversight committees such as the university's coordinating council.

One of the strategies identified in both the recruitment and retention plans was to increase the range of online offerings. From both incoming and continuing students there was a recognized need that more offerings could produce more momentum for the program. This effort met with concern from within the university because some faculty and departments were reluctant to expand into adult programs and particularly reluctant to move into online programs. Eventually, these reservations in the targeted professional disciplines were dispelled enough to provide the necessary number of online offerings so students could trust the program's viability. But that was made possible only by a continued emphasis on centralized responsibilities, rather than resorting to older notions of distributed operations. With attention to how RANA's mission might be realized through expansion of offerings, there was also attention to how offerings might become more relevant to adult students. Starting with the university's standardized writing placement exam, efforts were made to develop more relevance whenever possible. In this case, the placement test had always featured a writing

NEW DIRECTIONS FOR HIGHER EDUCATION • DOI:10.1002/he

prompt that was usually determined to be of interest to the traditional liberal arts students entering the university. With more centralized attention to adult online students, the writing program identified a specific prompt for incoming adult students that also had direct relevance to issues within Alaska. Further, texts and reading materials for the online writing courses were evaluated in relation to cultural relevance and online accessibility.

Drafted in spring 2006, RANA's recruitment and retention plans were more aspirational than data driven. They did, though, confirm the move toward centralized administration and establish a baseline from which to consider that transition. Whether by virtue of these plans and the administrative transition, or because of other factors, from 2005 to 2010, the RANA Program grew significantly, more than quadrupling overall FTE, doubling the number of Alaska Native participants, and improving retention rates. Perhaps just as significantly, the number of online offerings multiplied threefold. In the fall of 2010, 30 percent of undergraduate students (including those in the RANA Program) were taking one or more online course per semester, and success rates in those courses had improved.

The Future

In 2009–10, the RANA Program celebrated its tenth anniversary. With a compelling mission aligned to that of the institution's founding, the program had grown through both external sponsorship and internal commitment. Transitions in administrative patterns had mirrored the developments and needs of this growing adult program. Continuing to address the best ways to facilitate the needs within Alaska for adult programs, online offerings, and culturally responsive and relevant curriculum, the university is now embarked on yet another phase of administrative transition, and the RANA Program is again at the heart of institutional considerations. With growing interest from adult students for distance education, there is even greater need for centralized administration of offerings and services, so that adult students are met with timely, consistent, and accessible information. With increasing opportunities for e-learning, APU is having to reconfigure administrative responsibilities at the central level, shifting from a programmatic focus on distance education specifically for adult students to a more overarching concern for online learning across all educational offerings. And, with more Alaska Native students, the university is poised to develop Alaska Native–specific studies, aimed at both adult and traditional students. RANA was begun as an educational niche program—online, for adult students, and targeted to rural Alaska. In what seems a positive move, those somewhat discrete aspects are now being embraced more comprehensively across the university, and administrative patterns are once again in transition to support the new challenges and opportunities.

New Directions for Higher Education • DOI:10.1002/he

References

Alaska Pacific University. n.d. "About APU." Accessed June 24, 2012. http://www
.alaskapacific.edu/about-apu
Hayden, L. 2008. *A. History of Alaska Methodist University (1948–1977) and Alaska Pacific
University (1978–2008).* Anchorage: Commission on Archives and History, Alaska
Conference of the United Methodist Church.

*ESTHER BETH SULLIVAN is associate professor of communications and theatre,
chairperson of the Liberal Studies Department, and past director of the Distance
Education and Rural Alaska Native Adult Distance Education Programs at
Alaska Pacific University.*

*ROSANNE V. PAGANO is an instructor of writing at Alaska Pacific University and
a past director of APU's writing program.*

*Alaska Pacific University is located in Anchorage, Alaska, and enrolls about
550 students total with nontraditional programs in business, education, and
health services.*

4

The two-person staff of the adult program at Lipscomb University envisions a number of potential benefits of having a much larger staff. However, budget constraints and current staffing patterns oblige them to maintain a very centralized structure, and they rely greatly on colleagues in other offices across campus.

One Body, Many Parts:
An Adult Program Profile

Teresa Bagamery Clark

The Lipscomb University Adult Degree Program exemplifies how a centralized governance system can benefit nontraditional college students and promote cross-departmental interactions. However, such a programmatic organization also presents challenges to efficiency, because the adult program office depends on the time and expertise of other campus professionals to aid in fully serving the adult student. The adult program office at Lipscomb University (LU) resembles a small traditional department within the university more than it does a separate school or extension campus, as is the nature of some other college adult programs. This mostly centralized model also poses risks to the autonomy and self-sufficiency of an adult program office that does not independently house all the many functional segments necessary for its students' education. The Adult Degree Program (ADP) acts as the primary point of contact for all adult students but also coordinates with departments including student services and academic affairs. With adult student enrollment on the rise, the ADP perhaps works more diligently than ever before to meet its population's needs by serving as a liaison between these departments and the students.

Although the ADP office assumes only portions of the roles of other departments, it implements functions of several of the university's other offices in order to fulfill its role as the nontraditional learners' central hub. This is liberating in that one office can assist with multiple functions, but it is also a point of frustration as some tasks can be only partially completed before referring students to other campus personnel. The constraints of human and budgetary resources effectively prevent the office from adding the additional staff and faculty necessary to become a distributed system.

In addition to efficiency and autonomy, the Lipscomb University ADP must also reinforce its purpose on campus and serve a student population

NEW DIRECTIONS FOR HIGHER EDUCATION, no. 159, Fall 2012 © Wiley Periodicals, Inc.
Published online in Wiley Online Library (wileyonlinelibrary.com) • DOI:10.1002/he.20024

in a way that no other office can. Though a day may come when the university decides the ADP should function as a distributed program and move toward building the infrastructure to sustain that format, in the meantime the ADP is best suited to find a reasonable balance as a mostly centralized program. The key then is finding how best to partner with other staff and faculty while maximizing those services that can be provided within the walls of the adult office.

Background

The ADP is housed in the Adult Learning Department, which offers professional development opportunities such as noncredit test preparation on campus and continuing education units at conferences. For the purposes of this discussion, "ADP" is used to represent both the program and the department because administering the program is the department's central role. Although most students enrolled in this program are pursuing a degree, other nondegree-seeking students also enroll in the program.

The ADP currently provides the following degree options on an adult-friendly schedule that is a mix of evening, online, and weekend courses: bachelor of business administration in accounting, management, human resources, and information technology management; bachelor of social work; and bachelor of science degrees in interdisciplinary studies, K–6 (elementary) education, information technology applications, and law, justice, and society. The program also offers an online minor in applied ethics and an evening minor in psychology. All Lipscomb students, even those in the ADP, must complete an 18-credit minor as part of the requirement for graduation.

Classes are offered evenings and Saturdays in various formats with some hybrid (online and face-to-face) options. Courses are generally eight weeks in length with some shorter courses offered in the summer.

The ADP office, which is operated by a director, one administrative assistant, and two work-study students, is a one-stop shop for adult students from the point of inquiry to graduation. The director is the adviser for each ADP student. The office acts as a liaison between adult students and the rest of campus, functioning as students' "hands and feet" to complete their business during campus hours when they are working or caring for their children. The office also maintains connections with adult program alumni.

The program's primary role in the early days was helping students complete a degree they had begun at a previous time, but today students may complete an entire bachelor's degree in the evening format. Students may also earn a second bachelor's degree if they need a new direction of study for a career change or personal enrichment. The majors offered and the session lengths have evolved over the past twenty years, and during this time, the ADP has assumed a larger role in providing educational services to its students on campus.

New Directions for Higher Education • DOI:10.1002/he

In the spring of 2011, the ADP reached its highest enrollment at 201 students. In addition to internal efforts, the external environment of the recent recession, the post-9/11 GI Bill, and the growing need for a bachelor's degree to compete in the workforce all contributed to the program's overall growth. Enrollment increases were also helped by a first-to-second-year retention rate that rose to 84 percent. As the ADP finds itself achieving a record enrollment, the university is taking the opportunity to consider whether a centralized format best serves the parties involved.

Centralized Structure

The ADP office manages two main tasks: recruitment and retention. Of course, each of these broad issues involves several components, some of which require the collaboration of other departments on campus. Those offices with which the ADP most closely works include admissions, financial aid and student accounts, the registrar's office, and the academic colleges. The partnerships with these departments, including the roles the ADP plays, are discussed in detail in this section.

Recruiting new adult students had always belonged solely to the ADP office until admissions entered into a partnership with ADP in 2009. A new recruiter, employed by the admissions office, now focuses her efforts on adult students and meets weekly with the ADP director.

This partnership has proven to be greatly successful, because a recruiter provides both assistance and expertise to the Lipscomb University ADP's staff members. Meanwhile, the ADP office has remained involved in the application process. The recruiter attends education and employment fairs, and the program director makes campus visits to community colleges. The two departments coordinate their work on marketing efforts. Although inquiring students can contact the ADP office at any stage of the process for program-specific questions, informal transcript review, and academic advising, the admissions office conducts the official transcript review for transfer credit evaluation.

In addition to working with admissions, the ADP also relies on staff in the financial aid and student accounts offices to serve the adult students. The ADP director can view the student's financial aid award and provide basic details regarding specific types of aid; however, students desiring more information need to contact the financial aid office. No employee is designated as the sole ADP financial officer. Similarly, if students experience problems with their accounts, they must contact the student accounts office that serves all undergraduate and graduate students.

Whereas traditional undergraduates complete their own major-minor form to officially declare their degree intentions, the ADP office assumes all responsibility for completion of the adult students' forms. Adults need only sign their names on the forms. ADP students register for their own classes online.

The registrar's office issues the final approval for transfer credit. However, the ADP director secures department chairs' approval for major and minor credit on transfer credit approval forms and forwards those to the registrar. The ADP can also seek out course substitutions, and, with the e-mailed agreement of the department chair, pass those on to the registrar. In addition to approving and uploading transfer credit, the registrar's office also issues the approval for a student to graduate, ensuring all the course requirements have been met. ADP manages the students' files until the point of graduation, working with the academic departments on graduation verification.

The ADP office works very closely with the academic colleges and departments, especially those hosting the adult students' majors and minors: the College of Business; College of Education; Department of Social Work; Department of Information Technology and Computer Science; Institute for Law, Justice, and Society; Department of Psychology; and Department of History, Philosophy, and Political Science. The director works with department chairs to schedule evening, weekend, and online courses on a consistent basis so students can plan their course schedule up to a year ahead. The director also makes course requests from general education offices, such as math and English.

Arranging the schedule each semester involves e-mail, phone calls, and in-person conversations. The relationship between the ADP director and department chairs is extremely important because the adult students are not organized into cohorts. ADP cannot simply start students on a prescribed course of study in a lock-step manner. Instead, practically every student's schedule of courses differs from all the others. In order for ADP students to graduate in a timely fashion, the academic departments must regularly offer these courses throughout the year.

In addition to requesting courses, the ADP office works with department chairs to secure signatures on paperwork such as the major-minor declaration form, grade change forms, transfer credit evaluations, and other forms. Course substitutions among Lipscomb courses also involve requesting permission from the appropriate chair and then processing the granted permission with the registrar. The director also calls upon academic chairs to assist with events such as information sessions and orientation, so prospective and new students can get to know a faculty member in their major department. Finally, the academic departments have the responsibility to staff the evening, weekend, and online courses.

Challenges

Although partnerships often work well, collaborating within a centralized structure also presents challenges. If the adult learning office exercised complete control of the ADP, that is, operated in a distributed format, functions such as admissions, financial aid, accounts, registration, and academics

NEW DIRECTIONS FOR HIGHER EDUCATION • DOI:10.1002/he

would all reside in-house in terms of human resources and physical location. ADP would hold more decision-making authority instead of relying on the stretched capabilities of many other offices. The director would not need to rely on multiple departments and offices on campus to serve a single adult student. A new ADP student could move from inquiry to the first night of class by working with staff and faculty from one office, increasing smoothness and efficiency in the process. As it now stands, a new student may interact with five separate departments on campus, whether by phone, e-mail, or in person, before beginning classes.

Further, if these functions were all located in the same building, then paperwork could be processed more quickly and problems would be solved faster. The director could walk down the hall instead of across campus to meet with the financial aid officer, recruiter, or registrar. Collaboration could increase not only through proximity but because the staff in these positions would all be ADP employees and part of one team. Other than the recruiter, who works solely with adult students, the staff and faculty in the other campus offices that currently work with adult students could return to focusing on traditional undergraduates.

In terms of self-sufficiency and autonomy, the director could hire faculty to teach specifically for the ADP instead of depending on the department chairs to have professors available and willing to teach in the adult format. In addition, the ADP could add new majors to its offerings if it did not need to rely on department chairs' approval to provide the classes or agreement to supply the faculty. This would not only provide freedom for the ADP to respond to its students' needs and market trends but also remove a burden from the academic departments currently charged with these responsibilities. Of course, given the current pressures on human resources, if Lipscomb University adopted a distributed structure, additional staff and faculty would need to be hired or current campus employees would need to be reclassified to work for the ADP.

Benefits

Although understandable challenges exist, the centralized structure of the ADP also presents positive outcomes. First, with the very small size of the current ADP office staff, ADP could not exist in a distributed structure. The current staff of two already must shift hats multiple times throughout the day. In this way, the office as it presently stands must be able to work with the university financial aid office and registrar's office, because ADP does not have the resources or expertise to perform all those duties itself. Further, additions to staff and faculty would be required to sustain an extension school or college for the adult programs. Since ADP does not have the budget to hire its own employees for all these functions, it is fortunate that other offices and academic colleges are willing to share their expertise and time. Although the ADP may wish for increased autonomy, its ability to function efficiently would suffer if the office suddenly assumed all the responsibilities necessary to serve its students.

In addition, the ADP possesses positive and strong relationships with the offices of admissions, financial aid, student accounts, registrar, and academic department. Representatives in each of these areas willingly meet and coordinate with the ADP director and administrative assistant and are most often able to accommodate ADP requests. Staff and faculty in the other offices graciously offer their time to assist adult students. If there is a future transition from a centralized to distributed structure, this change should not be seen as a negative reflection on the university employees in the other departments.

Conclusion

Over the past five years, the ADP has shown enrollment growth and increased student retention, so the centralized structure is certainly not preventing growth in student numbers. However, based on this discussion of challenges of centralization, a distributed model may be able to improve recruitment and retention. The ADP has demonstrated that despite a small staff, a vibrant program is possible. At present, the key is to strike a balance between the current centralized structure and the potential for distribution to promote efficiency and self-sufficiency, not for the purpose of independence, but for the improvement of student services and program management. At the same time, the ADP wishes to maintain healthy relationships with other campus personnel and departments, regardless of its own structure. The other offices would find more time to work with the remainder of the student body if adult students were no longer part of their concern; however, they have been accommodating under a centralized format in which their cooperation is essential. In addition, the ADP continues to perform as many roles as possible in the educational lives of its students to best serve adult students and reinforce the relevance of the program on campus. A stronger ADP, regardless of its governance structure, is the best solution for students, the university as a whole, and the ADP itself.

TERESA BAGAMERY CLARK *is the director of new program research and design for the College of Professional Studies at Lipscomb University in Nashville, Tennessee.*

Lipscomb University enrolls about 3,000 students. The nontraditional programs, launched in 1991, enroll about 200 in undergraduate programs focused on business, education, and social work.

NEW DIRECTIONS FOR HIGHER EDUCATION • DOI:10.1002/he

North Park University's adult program has moved steadily from a centralized governance structure toward a more distributed structure in many ways. The School of Adult Learning hires its own faculty, some of whom are full time in the adult program. The school also has autonomy over academic policy. Ultimately, this academic autonomy has fostered more effective and meaningful integration of the School of Adult Learning into the wider institution of North Park University.

Academic Autonomy for Adult Degree Programs: Independence with Integration

Judson Curry

In *Systems of Excellence in Adult Higher Education*, Mark Smith (2007) argues that "the most successful adult-oriented programs . . . are those that have an administrative structure of independence"(20). Smith encourages academic leaders to free adult degree programs from dependent administrative structures and to create "separate but coequal" systems for every function of adult degree programs—from enrollment management to library services, from faculty to budgeting. Many directors of adult degree programs would happily embrace such a move toward independence and freedom, but clearly this sort of paradigm shift in higher education requires commitment at the highest levels of leadership within an institution. Rarely does such a massive institutional shift occur in a single instant. Given the challenges and barriers in pursuit of independent administrative structures for adult degree programs, what strategies can adult degree program directors and administrators employ to lay the groundwork for greater autonomy within the institution? And what form should administrative independence take?

This chapter examines the development of North Park University's School of Adult Learning and makes a case for the pursuit of academic autonomy as key to both academic excellence and innovative flexibility. Academic autonomy includes decentralized or distributed control within the adult degree program over curriculum, faculty, academic policy, and assessment of learning. One of the chief benefits of this academic autonomy, however, is the opportunity for more transformational integration into the institution. Academic autonomy allows the adult degree program to build the cultural and social capital necessary to effect change within the institution.

New Directions for Higher Education, no. 159, Fall 2012 © Wiley Periodicals, Inc.
Published online in Wiley Online Library (wileyonlinelibrary.com) • DOI:10.1002/he.20025

Although the administrative structure of the School of Adult Learning includes elements from a variety of administrative models, the most critical development over the history of this adult program has been the consolidation of academic and curricular independence. North Park's adult degree program has evolved from a centralized structure to a distributed model where the adult degree program is an academically independent division of the university. More than any other factor, this development of academic autonomy has improved academic rigor and student achievement of learning outcomes, increased credibility within the institution, and enhanced curricular responsiveness to market and occupational trends. As an independent, distributed academic unit of the university, an adult degree program can achieve both excellence and innovation without sacrificing its alignment with institutional mission, vision, and values. By creating a recognized and credible place at the table of academic leadership within the college or university, the adult program can achieve freedom to innovate in the present and access to influence the future of the institution.

Independence: What Kind? What Cost?

Independence as an administrative goal may be envisioned as a fully *distributed or decentralized* structure for the adult degree program. In this model, the adult degree program contains all necessary functions within itself: curriculum, instruction, marketing, enrollment, financial management, and support services. No function is shared with the traditional undergraduate program, and the adult program is entirely autonomous. This vision of a fully self-sufficient administrative structure may seem almost utopian to many adult program administrators who are toiling to free their programs from the restrictions of traditional undergraduate paradigms. As with many utopian visions, though, there may be hidden risks.

Complete independence and decentralization of all functions of an adult degree program pose an attractive prospect. There are two chief dangers, however, in the "separate but coequal" model proposed by Smith. The first is the brute fact that separate units within an institution are rarely truly equal. In a college or university divided into two disconnected administrative and academic structures—one for traditional, four-year, college-age students and another for adult, nontraditional students—one of these two units will experience marginalization, whether actual or perceived. Intentionally or unintentionally, the institution's leadership will bestow favored status on one of these units. That status may shift as the leadership changes or as the reputation and revenue of the programs rise and fall, but it seems unlikely that the desired coequal status can be effectively balanced. This is especially true for institutions that have historically identified themselves with traditional college-age students and programs. That identity is likely to remain linked to the past, giving centrality to the traditional undergraduate program, even while future viability may depend on the adult student population.

The second danger, perhaps a more significant danger for smaller, independent colleges and universities, is the loss of institutional integrity. An institution that houses two distinct and disassociated academic and administrative units may struggle to maintain a unified mission and vision. Without integration of all units of the institution, resources and opportunities for more effective engagement with the institution's mission may be lost. It is not only the adult degree programs that need to be creative and entrepreneurial to respond to social and economic shifts; all areas within the college or university must cultivate new approaches to teaching, learning, and serving students of all kinds. In order for smaller, independent institutions to successfully pursue their missions, adult degree programs must be integrated into and have a stake in that mission.

Given these risks, as well as the practical challenge of achieving complete decentralized independence, what other models are available? Which elements or functions of the adult degree program can be most usefully moved toward autonomy? Where should administrators choose to focus their energy? And what strategies should they employ?

Starting at the Margins

Many, if not most, adult degree completion programs begin at the margins of their home college or university. The marginal status of adult undergraduate degree programs is a regularly recurring theme, almost a cliché. Lee Bash (2003) begins his assessment of the impact of adult learners on higher education by asserting that adult learning programs "are seldom fully integrated into the mainstream of the institution by either faculty or administration" (3). A 2006 analysis of the strategies of adult degree program planners at "small, private, nonprofit, higher education institutions" highlights the challenges of attempting to move adult programs "from being seen as marginal to the mission of the university . . . to being seen as equally important as those [programs] aimed at the needs of traditional-age students" (Watkins and Tisdell 2006, 145).

This marginal position is often closely associated with a *centralized* administrative structure with regard to the adult degree program, in which each component of the program is controlled or administered by offices or units serving the entire institution. Often, in smaller traditional liberal arts colleges and universities, these other offices are asked to support an adult program that they do not fully understand or value. There may be an administrator with nominal responsibility for the adult degree program, but that individual can be locked in continual negotiation with faculty and staff who have no particular stake in the adult student population. This sort of centralized administrative structure can ensure that a program remains on the margins of the college or university, operating with little visibility and without power of its own.

This was the case at North Park College in 1991, the inaugural year of the GOAL (Gains of Adult Learning) Program, an accelerated adult degree

NEW DIRECTIONS FOR HIGHER EDUCATION • DOI:10.1002/he

completion program. North Park, originally founded to provide education in language, business, and religion to adult Swedish immigrants, had for many years built its identity as a traditional four-year liberal arts college. The college had previously experimented with extension programs for non-traditional students, with varying degrees of success, but GOAL was a new attempt to develop an academically respectable and financially profitable adult program.

Initially, the GOAL administrative structure consisted of a single director housed in the Division of Social Sciences. This director, lacking faculty status and hired just weeks before the first student cohort was scheduled to begin, faced significant faculty resistance. The program did have the support of the president, however, who recognized the revenue opportunities of an adult degree program. One major was offered, Organizational Management, using a packaged curriculum purchased from a consultant. Instructors for GOAL classes were recruited from the traditional North Park faculty, who taught GOAL classes as overload, with the addition of adjuncts as needed. One admissions recruiter was hired to work with prospective adult undergraduate students.

This highly centralized model left the GOAL Program dependent for its success on individuals, departments, and offices whose primary responsibilities and allegiances lay elsewhere. Without faculty status, academic authority, or a supportive academic department, the GOAL director lacked cultural capital in the institution. As a new arrival to the North Park community, she also lacked the social capital of those embedded in a network of established friendships and allies. Even the program's physical space, two windowless rooms off a noisy lobby area and far from other faculty and staff offices, illustrated the marginal status of the program.

Building Cultural and Social Capital from the Margins

For adult degree program administrators, the process of negotiating the transition from a centralized model of administration to a more distributed administrative structure requires a long-term investment strategy. Watkins and Tisdell (2006) employ Bourdieu's (1986) concepts of cultural and social capital, particularly applied within academic institutions, as a tool for understanding how adult degree program administrators negotiate power in order to move "adult degree programs from the margins closer to the center" (Watkins and Tisdell, 136).

For Bourdieu (1986), cultural capital operates at the level of worldview, as a "set of constraints" that provides a foundation for an individual's comprehension of and success in the dominant society. Cultural capital is gained not so much through education as through an unconscious process of "inheritance," and, in fact, cultural capital serves as the prerequisite for success in formal education. In its institutionalized form within higher education, cultural capital is most visible in academic degrees, titles, rankings, and other forms of institutional recognition, but it is also the ground on which our understanding of higher education and its institutions is built. This helps to explain why nontraditional adult degree programs struggle to make a place for themselves in institutions with a more traditional liberal arts identity. The nature and orientation of these programs challenge the accepted value of cultural capital within higher education.

Similarly, social capital names the formal and informal networks and relationships that create trust between individuals. Social capital, according to Robert Putnam (2000), both bonds us to those in our current networks and creates bridges to new individuals and networks. Within any complex organization, such as a college or university, in which power is dispersed across many stakeholders, an individual's ability to leverage social capital is vital to work effectively.

Lack of cultural and social capital is both a cause and an effect of the marginal position of adult degree programs. Lacking cultural and social capital, adult programs are forced to operate at the margins with inhibited ability, in turn, to develop and invest cultural and social capital.

However, some reflective observations on developments within North Park University's adult degree program suggest that there are effective strategies for building cultural and social capital in order to create a more independent role for an adult degree program.

Identify and Build Institutionally Recognized Links with Supportive Faculty. Several years after the start of North Park's adult degree program, the director was able to recruit a sympathetic faculty member to assist with the development of a new major. The successful launch of this new major created an opportunity for this faculty member, who valued the principles of adult learning, to shift her position so that she became the first faculty member appointed specifically to the adult program. This small gain in cultural capital laid the groundwork for the future appointment of additional faculty specifically assigned to the adult program.

Seek Opportunities to Leverage the Entrepreneurial Nature of Adult Degree Program to Pilot New Initiatives for the Institution. North Park's adult program has positioned itself intentionally to serve as a proving ground for online learning and new efforts in the assessment of student learning. Not only does this emphasize the value of the program to university leadership, but successes in these new initiatives demonstrate academic excellence to traditional faculty.

Build Collaborative Bridges to Other Departments and with Other Faculty. During the recent development of a major in criminal justice for adult students, it became clear that there was significant interest among traditional undergraduates in such a major. This allowed the adult program faculty and administration to collaborate with faculty in the traditional program to create shared courses.

New Directions for Higher Education • DOI: 10.1002/he

The School of Adult Learning: Academic Autonomy

Now, twenty years after its launch, the GOAL Program has become the School of Adult Learning. Within the administrative structure of the university, the School of Adult Learning exists alongside the School of Business and Nonprofit Management, the School of Nursing, the School of Education, the School of Music, and the College of Arts and Sciences. A dean leads each of these units, and the deans' council, guided by the provost, provides leadership for the entire university. Within the School of Adult Learning, four full-time faculty members (two tenure-track, two professional) oversee the eight different majors. Four full-time master's-level academic advisers also have teaching loads built into their contracts. As a result, about half of all adult degree program courses are taught by full-time faculty and staff within the School of Adult Learning. The School of Adult Learning develops and reviews its own curriculum, as well as all academic policy related to transfer credits and academic standing of adult undergraduate students. Faculty appointments and evaluations are conducted by the dean of the School of Adult Learning, and faculty members represent the school on the university faculty senate and in other university-wide committees.

The School of Adult Learning still faces some challenges associated with a centralized model of administration. The single recruiter for the adult undergraduate program is housed within the university's office of admissions, which also exercises control over the budget for marketing and recruiting. A university-wide student services office administers many student services, including student accounts, financial aid, and career services. School of Adult Learning advisers often function as liaisons to these offices on behalf of students.

However, over the course of its growth, the School of Adult Learning has focused its efforts on developing its academic place within the university, rather than pursuing a distributed strategy for recruiting and student service functions. This has not necessarily been the result of an intentional plan. A confluence of particular contexts, opportunities, individuals, and challenges has shaped the history and development of this adult program. The consequence, however, is that the School of Adult Learning has gained recognition, credibility, and representation within the institution, which ensures both independence for the adult degree program and integration with other university units. Not only does the School of Adult Learning have the freedom to create new courses and majors in response to new opportunities and market demands, but it also has a role in shaping larger institutional developments, including the revision of general education outcomes, attitudes toward and policies for transfer students, and long-range strategic planning.

NEW DIRECTIONS FOR HIGHER EDUCATION • DOI:10.1002/he

Lessons from the Margins

Marginality may be seen as a gift. "Marginality allows for creativity and responsiveness to changing needs; indeed, the entrepreneurial quality of much of adult education would not be possible if it were encumbered with large bureaucratic structures" (Merriam and Brockett 1997, 111). Bash (2003) echoes this notion: "Because [continuing education programs] tend to be institutionally marginalized and usually lack the financial security of more established programs, they are more likely to be at risk so that their very existence relies on their flexibility, responsiveness, and willingness to think less conventionally" (179). The uncertainty and freedom that comes with marginal territory can drive innovation.

Adult programs seek decentralized, independent administrative structures in order to maintain these marginal characteristics of freedom and flexibility. And yet, although the pursuit of complete "separate but coequal" independence can produce greater efficiency and effectiveness within the adult program unit, it can also result in continued marginalization and separation from the institution. Without intentional integration into the institution, adult programs become isolated. As a result, we lose the larger opportunities to reshape our colleges and universities into more innovative and entrepreneurial institutions.

The margins might also be seen as a place of service. Those of us involved in adult higher education have a unique service mission. We advocate on behalf of adult students' needs. We attempt to remove institutional obstacles from the paths of adult learners. Our efforts toward these ends drive us to build decentralized, independent administrative structures dedicated to supporting adult learners. But the pursuit of institutional resources and credibility should always be in the service of the larger institutional mission, not merely to achieve success, power, or recognition for the adult unit only. Our integration within the entire institution can contribute to a deeper commitment to service across the college or university.

It may be that adult program administrators assume that successful movement from a centralized administrative model to a distributed model will coincide with an equivalent movement from the margins of the institution toward the center. But radical decentralization may not result in a more significant role within the college or university. In fact, it may be that the language of "center" and "margin" is not the most useful method for conceiving the place of adult programs in smaller independent colleges and universities whose identities have been closely tied to traditional-age student populations. Nearly every unit, division, school, or department in most smaller, independent colleges and universities struggles with the fear of being marginalized. Few academic units would claim to be securely at the center of their institutions, but if everyone worries that someone else is closer to the center, then what are the consequences for the institution? The margin–center metaphor suggests competition for scarce resources in which only one academic unit can hold the center, while all others are relegated to the margins.

If the pursuit of independent and decentralized administrative structures is undertaken as a tactic for amassing power within the institution, then it is surely a misguided goal. The outcome of such a successful battle for resources and control may be greater independence for the adult degree program, but only at the cost of integration within the institution and opportunities for a more significant institutional impact. Adult degree programs should work to develop independent administrative structures, but with the larger goal of influencing colleges and universities. A strategy of building academic autonomy through investment in cultural and social capital is one path toward independence and integration.

References

Bash, L. 2003. *Adult Learners in the Academy*. Bolton, MA: Anker.

Bourdieu, P. 1986. "The Forms of Capital." In *Handbook of Theory and Research for the Sociology of Education*, edited by J. Richardson, 241–258. New York: Greenwood.

Merriam, S., and R. Brockett. 1997. *The Profession and Practice of Adult Education*. San Francisco: Jossey-Bass.

Putnam, R. 2000. *Bowling Alone: The Collapse and Revival of American Community*. New York: Simon & Schuster.

Smith, M. A. 2007. "Administration of Adult Programs: Governance Is Key." In *Systems of Excellence in Adult Higher Education*, edited by S. Drury, 20–28. Marion, IN: Triangle Publishing.

Watkins, B. J., and E. J. Tisdell. 2006. "Negotiating the Labyrinth from Margin to Center: Adult Degree Program Administrators as Program Planners within Higher Education Institutions." *Adult Education Quarterly* 56(2): 134–159.

JUDSON CURRY *is associate director of the School of Adult Learning of North Park University in Chicago.*

North Park University enrolls approximately 3,000 students. Nontraditional programs, launched in 1991, enroll about 250 in eight undergraduate majors.

A member of the graduate faculty at Indiana Wesleyan University reviews the history of adult education among private institutions. Her overview notes the effects of adult programs on students, faculty, curriculum development, institutional mission, and organizational behavior.

The Impact of Adult Degree Programs on the Private College or University

Pamela A. Giles

Those of us who work within adult higher education know there is something unique about our perspective on academic life. Employed in the adult education arena in one capacity or another since 1993, I have had the privilege of working at an institution with a small adult program and an institution with a very large adult program. As I worked I discovered that the adult programs were somehow changing the institutions themselves. The best way I found to describe what I was seeing was that adding an adult program into the traditional academic setting is akin to a retiree gaining custody of a two-year-old. The energy and resources required to manage this new addition are shocking, and the elder siblings may resent the intrusion.

I observed and listened in the various venues in which I operated, but I realized I couldn't quite put my finger on what was happening. I became so curious about these issues that I decided to conduct a research investigation. What follows is a summary of what I learned about ways adult degree programs have an impact on their host institutions.

Introduction

Private liberal arts colleges and universities, both faith based and secular, represent a vibrant, viable alternative within higher education. Their smaller size and independence from some aspects of state oversight allow them a degree of flexibility and adaptability not so common among their public counterparts, providing opportunities to respond to changes from their constituents and the culture at large. The addition of adult degree programs (ADPs) has been one of the most popular and successful innovations affecting private colleges and universities. By offering education at times and locations accessible to the working adult and compressing the time required to

New Directions for Higher Education, no. 159, Fall 2012 © Wiley Periodicals, Inc.
Published online in Wiley Online Library (wileyonlinelibrary.com) • DOI:10.1002/he.20026

complete a degree, these institutions have tapped into a large market. In fact, private, four-year institutions offer more distance degree programs than do public four-year institutions (Maehl 2004).

The same distinctive features that make ADPs successful also create difficulties for college and university administrators when they try to integrate these innovative systems into existing academic structures. The typical outcome is a single academic organization with two different internal structures: one to address the needs of the traditional degree programs and one to address the needs of the ADPs. In the long run, this internal compartmentalizing may have an adverse effect on the internal, unseen structures of the college or university, which, in turn, may affect the quality and services associated with the adult degree programs (Bash 2003; Husson and Kennedy 2003; Singh and Martin 2004; Sissel, Hansman, and Kasworm 2001).

A Brief History of Adult Degree Programs

Alternative education options for American adults have been present since the early eighteenth-century's public "Thursday lectures" in Puritan New England. The end of World War II brought adult learners en masse to higher education, and these new learners surprised administrators and faculty with their ability, wisdom, and experience (Maehl 2004). In the 1970s, government policies related to financial aid and the promotion of vocational education led to the development of education programs for adults (Husson and Kennedy 2003).

By the 1980s, a growing group of students who had not completed bachelor degrees wanted to finish college, and those who had bachelor degrees now wanted graduate degrees. Institutions responded by developing innovative programs tailored to the unique learning and life needs of working adults. Adult degree programs were born, allowing an adult student to transfer credits, enroll with a cohort group of fellow students, take accelerated classes, and earn a bachelor's degree in two years or less. Small independent college campuses suffering from enrollment shortfalls were quick to adopt the ADP format, and the number of adult students taking classes for credit grew 171 percent between 1970 and 1991 (Sissel, Hansman, and Kasworm 2001).

The 1990s saw the rise of corporate and for-profit colleges and universities. The accompanying explosion in computer technology and the introduction of the Internet led to the development of online education. The statistics for growth in online adult education are astonishing. In 2001, online enrollment was 350,000 with $1.75 billion in revenue (Huber and Lowry 2003). By 2005, online enrollment had hit 3.2 million, and revenue was $7.1 billion (Foster and Carnevale 2007).

Numbers like these are inspiring for administrators seeking enrollment growth. But some private liberal arts colleges and universities view the addition of ADPs as an easy remedy for their financial challenges without taking into account the quantity and quality of support services required to sustain such ventures (Balzer 1996; Terrell 1990). Adding adult programs to traditional liberal arts colleges brings significant change, along with implications for the entire institution. "These implications need to be seriously considered, if not for the sake of the program, then for the sake of the institution-at-large" (Balzer 1996, 141).

The Impact of Adult Degree Programs

A broad review of the literature yields five general areas in which adult degree programs have an impact on the traditional private college or university: (1) students, (2) faculty, (3) curriculum, (4) mission, and (5) organizational behavior.

Students. Today's college students have become unexpected power brokers within the academy. They are consumers of education, often shopping online for the program they want, the credits they want, at the price and location they prefer. Adult students desire three things: (1) a program that is accessible, relevant, and predictable, (2) a degree structure that pushes them through to completion, and (3) a sense of connectedness to fellow students in a caring community (Kasworm 2003). They look for emotional support, personal connections, and personalized educational services to help them survive the inevitable emotional, personal, and life challenges they will encounter while they are enrolled. They view accelerated learning programs as more customized and supportive compared to their previous experiences with traditional learning systems.

Program viability depends on the use of sophisticated marketing because students are now choosing from a wide variety of options. This requires new technology and new organizational structures and administrators, resulting in increased cost to the institution.

Faculty. Adult degree programs often use working professionals as adjunct faculty for a majority of their courses, thereby significantly cutting costs. However, adjunct faculty may not only have a decreased commitment to the school in general, but they may also have less understanding of the institutional mission and how to enact it (Flory 2002). Therefore, great attention needs to be given to the hiring process and faculty development to ensure alignment with the school's mission and to assist the working professional to take on the new role of teacher (Smith 2007). Traditional faculty have often been slow to accept the academic validity or quality of ADPs, grudgingly accepting adult program faculty as a necessary part of academic life without according them the respect and collegiality they offer to their traditional peers (Cranch 1999; Husson and Kennedy 2003; Pearce 1992).

Curriculum. Typical curricular modifications made for ADPs include being more degree focused than course focused and compressing course content into an accelerated time frame (Flory 2002). Adult students appreciate courses that are designed to connect course content with their real-world experiences. It is normal for a program's curriculum to be standardized into preformatted modules with predetermined objectives, assignments, and classroom activities. Whereas some instructors decry the loss of academic freedom, others applaud the attempts at quality control in multiple classroom locations that may span the globe.

An institution's traditional campus-based faculty may be a significant obstacle to the success of ADPs (Husson and Kennedy 2003). The popularity of ADPs along with the demands from employers and the changing culture have led to a shift in curricular emphasis in the academy from a liberal arts perspective to one that is more vocational and professional. This shift has caused a great deal of debate within both religious and secular institutions, with many traditional faculty decrying the loss of emphasis on teaching students how to think and nontraditional faculty championing the preparation of graduates with job skills for the twenty-first century (Badley 1998; Blevins 1998; Martin 1986; McMurtrie 2000). Although they may appreciate the increased revenue, traditional faculty often assume the revisions made to accommodate the adult learner result in a weakened curriculum and negatively affect the credibility of the school. Research, however, has demonstrated that ADP outcomes are equivalent and sometimes superior to those of traditional programs (Bash 2003; Donaldson and Graham 2002).

Mission. Apart from the financial benefits, one of the strongest motivations for a college to begin an ADP may be to expand the institution's mission to adult students (Winston 1999). Stakeholders increase once adult education is added. Colleges and universities are required to listen to the needs of students and their current and potential employers as they review programs. Corporations that are willing to fund student tuition costs may request changes that cause an institution to reexamine, modify, or reaffirm its mission. Adjunct faculty who do not fully understand or even support the mission of a private college or university may further challenge an institution's sense of its mission.

However, there is little in the literature to indicate that adults select an adult degree program at a private college or university *because* of a stated mission. They select it because it is accessible and meets the needs previously outlined.

Maintaining a revenue-generating enterprise while remaining a nonprofit organization presents additional challenges. Although higher education must take on some characteristics of a business, administrators need integrity and sensitivity to keep a rapidly changing institution from weakening its stated mission.

There may be an alternative perspective to this issue. It has been documented that adult learners experience life transitions before, during, and after enrollment in an adult degree program (Merriam 2005). The ability of a private college or university and its faculty and staff to mentor adults as they make these transitions may enable a positive alignment with the institution's mission. The true value of the contribution of an education at such institutions may not be identified until much later and then perceived as only one of many elements affecting change in alumni behaviors, attitudes, and abilities.

Organizational Behavior. The impact of ADPs is also felt in the organizational behavior of the academic institution itself, in areas such as administrative structure, revenues, and productivity (Sparks 1994). ADPs require a different type of administrative structure, because the majority of programs are not semester based and do not run continuously year-round. Additionally, new cohorts of students begin the program at various times throughout the year. The traditional position of chair or dean is not usually designed to deal simultaneously with the demands of traditional and nontraditional programs and their students (Sparks 1994).

There are two distinct administrative areas related to adult programs: operations and academics. Operations deals with financial aid, accounting, enrollment, recruitment, textbook distribution, online support, technical support, and other related services. Academics deals with admission and progress, revision of existing programs, the launch of new programs, hiring and assigning of faculty, assessment and accreditation, and student issues (Drury, Griffin, and Hahn 2007; Smith 2007). Schools initiating ADPs may be unprepared for the number of people required to successfully support the needs and expectations of adult students.

> Administration of an adult college requires a team of faculty with expertise in adult learning theory as well as administrators with operational understanding of how to administer multisite campuses, recruitment of students and faculty, delivery of resources, and student services. (Smith 2007, 21)

These unique needs often lead to two distinct, rather fragmented areas within the college or university, one designed to deal with the unique needs of adult programs and their students, and the other with traditional programs and their students. Kofman and Senge (1995) speak to how this fragmentation within an organization leads to "independent and often warring fiefdoms" instead of cooperating "with a sense of shared aspiration" (18).

ADPs can be quite profitable. "The business model associated with adult degree programs, which focuses on the revenue they produce and the contribution margins they generate, has moved from the periphery of the institution to a more central position" (Matkin 2004, 61). Perhaps one of the most sensitive topics is how the college or university manages the revenue from these programs. According to Matkin (2004) the ADPs generate millions of dollars of revenue each year and turn over the majority of it to the institutions' general funds, essentially subsidizing the education of and support services for residential students. The term "cash cow" characterizes a general attitude toward ADPs (Bash, 2003).

> The fact that one category of student (working adults) is subsidizing another category of student (residential students) rarely is discussed or debated, and when the issue is raised, such a subsidy is justified on the unexamined ground that working adults are better able to pay for their education than are residential students. (Matkin 2004, 63)

Administrators of adult degree programs need to ensure that adequate revenues are retained to sustain current and growing operations and to manage research and development for new endeavors.

This leads to the larger issue of productivity. "Continuing education is the unit on campus that has traditionally had its finger on the pulse of the marketplace and has learned how to bridge the gap between the university and the rest of the community" (Baden, as cited in Bash 2003, 22). Deans and directors of nontraditional adult programs are responsible for revenue generation, are expected to be conscious of changes and trends in the market and to respond with innovative programs, and to do all this with limited authority (Bash 2003; Sparks 1994).

However, the whole idea of entrepreneurialism is foreign to many traditional faculty members, who have found the whole issue "tawdry and suspect" (Crow, as cited in Bash 2003, 22). Some argue that the status of the college or university has changed. "The emphasis has moved away from one based on providing a forum for intellectualism and well-roundedness through science and the liberal arts toward a more corporate model that encourages outcome measures defined in terms of career potential and vocation preparation" (Ilsley 2004, 68).

So how does a private liberal arts institution structure itself to develop external awareness and internal responsiveness in order to facilitate an environment necessary for adult degree programs? The perspectives of organizational systems theorists and social psychologists are valuable in exploring this question.

Institutions as Systems

Colleges and universities are unique organizational systems (Halpin and Croft 1963). Until recently, universities appear to have traditionally functioned as closed systems, perceiving themselves as stand-alone entities, unaffected by environmental influences and analyzing their problems without reference to their external environment.

However, changes in student expectations, external culture, and technology have steered institutions to change their focus to one of an open system, and it now becomes necessary for a college or university to keep tabs on environmental changes, choosing if, when, and how to adapt with energies and resources focused on defining and maintaining a steady state of equilibrium. Katz and Kahn (1978) state the following:

Quantitative growth calls for supportive subsystems of a specialized character not necessary when the system was smaller. In the second place, there is a point where quantitative changes produce a qualitative difference in the functioning of a system. *A small college that triples its size is no longer the same institution in terms of the relation between its administration and faculty, relations among the various academic departments, or the nature of its instruction* [emphasis added]. (28)

Organizations that function in an environment typified by change and instability must reorganize to be effective and to be able to plan, make decisions, and resolve conflicts (Katz and Associates 1999; Owens 2001; Senge and others 1999). They require fairly flexible structures, emphasizing vertical communications instead of lateral communications, expert power instead of hierarchical power, exchanging information instead of giving direction, and loosely defined duties (Owens 2001).

The innovative organization gains new information about its environment and its culture by living and interacting on the border between the two worlds. The ability to monitor and identify changes allows the organization to generate new rules of operation when older rules become ineffective. Senge and others (1999) are quick to point out that significant growth and change do not always happen overnight. The familiar analogy of the boiled frog illustrates that sometimes change happens gradually; and in fact, the gradual change can be the most deceptive and lethal to an organization. Staffing ratios that were once more than adequate no longer fit the bill in the face of significant growth, and an organization that has become used to enjoying profits resulting from this growth can sometimes overlook the fact that it is requiring much more work from the same number of people.

But external positioning means nothing if internal processes do not follow suit. According to Kanter (1995), an adult degree program within a private college or university requires three kinds of speed to function effectively: innovation speed—"creating the future by developing new products and services that transform how everybody else in this industry must operate"; processing speed—"the time it takes for a change to process through the organization"; and recovery speed—"the time it takes to respond to and fix problems" (79–80).

This is not the world of the traditional academy, where life has an unhurried, more orderly pace, and where things are slow to change. This is the busy world of adult education—where the needs of adult students and their employers can quickly change and where those who market and offer adult education have to keep their fingers on the pulse of a rapidly changing world. Adult degree programs require administrative structures that allow them to function efficiently and respond effectively.

Summary

From its beginnings in Colonial America, private higher education has weathered a series of identity crises and now finds itself with the ability to innovate and adapt to society's changing demands, becoming one of the most popular of college options for today's students and their families. However, these changes have not come without their challenges. The world of adult degree programs has forever altered the face of private, faith-based and secular colleges and universities. Whether the competition is between institutions or within them, adult education is affecting all areas of the organization. Research is needed to study the impact of adult degree programs on the structure and behavior of a private college or university. As areas of challenge are identified, educational leaders will be able to make better decisions to improve their institution's effectiveness, have a positive impact on the total lives of students, and provide an environment that allows all employees to thrive in their given areas of expertise.

Surrounding all of this is the need to design organizational structures that simultaneously preserve the culture of the older, traditional academy while ensuring its younger sibling has the necessary resources to thrive and adapt to changing societal demands.

References

Badley, K. 1998. "Trends in Christian Higher Education." *Faith Today* 6: 41–47.

Balzer, W. 1996. "The Utilization of the Principles of Good Practice in Adult Degree Completion Programs." Unpublished dissertation, Northern Arizona University.

Bash, L. 2003. "Adult Learners: Why They Are Important to the 21st Century College or University." *Journal of Continuing Higher Education* 51(3): 18–26.

Blevins, D. 1998. "Denominational Identity and Higher Education: Formation and Discernment." *Christian Education Journal* 2: 111–122.

Cranch, E. 1999. "Competition or Collaboration: Survival Strategies for Continuing Higher Education." *Journal of Continuing Higher Education* 47(2): 2–14.

Donaldson, J. E., and S. W. Graham. 2002. "Accelerated Degree Programs: Design and Policy Implications." *Journal of Continuing Higher Education* 50(2): 2–13.

Drury, S., T. Griffin, and A. Hahn. 2007. "Innovative Systems in Student Services." In *Systems of Excellence*, edited by S. Drury, 44–48. Marion, IN: Triangle Publishing.

Flory, R. 2002. "Intentional Change and the Maintenance of Mission: The Impact of Adult Education Programs on School Mission at Two Evangelical Colleges." *Review of Religious Research* 43(4): 349–368.

Foster, A., and D. Carnevale. 2007. "Distance Education Goes Public." *Chronicle of Higher Education* 53(34): A49. Accessed June 24, 2012. http://chronicle.com/article/Distance-Education-Goes-Public/25893/.

Halpin, A., and D. Croft. 1963. *The Organizational Climate of Schools*. Chicago: University of Chicago Press.

Huber, H., and J. Lowry. 2003. "Meeting the Needs of Consumers: Lessons from Postsecondary Environments." *New Directions for Adult and Continuing Education*, no. 100: 79–88.

Husson, W., and T. Kennedy. 2003. "Developing and Maintaining Accelerated Degree Programs within Traditional Institutions." *New Directions for Adult and Continuing Education*, no. 97: 51–61.

Ilsley, P. 2004. "Adult Education Departments in the Entrepreneurial Age." *New Directions for Adult and Continuing Education*, no. 104: 67–75.

Kanter, R. 1995. "Mastering Change." In *Learning Organizations: Developing Cultures for Tomorrow's Workplace*, edited by S. Chawla and J. Renesch, 71–83. Portland, OR: Productivity Press.

Kasworm, C. 2003. "From the Adult Student's Perspective: Accelerated Degree Programs." *New Directions for Adult and Continuing Education*, no. 97: 17–27.

Katz, D., and R. Kahn. 1978. *The Social Psychology of Organizations*. New York: John Wiley & Sons.

Katz, R., and Associates. 1999. *Dancing with the Devil: Information Technology and the New Competition in Higher Education*. San Francisco: Jossey-Bass.

Kofman, F., and P. Senge. 1995. "Communities of Commitment: The Heart of Learning Organizations." In *Learning Organizations: Developing Cultures for Tomorrow's Workplace*, edited by S. Chawla and J. Renesch, pp. 15–43. Portland, OR: Productivity Press.

Maehl, W. 2004. "Adult Degrees and the Learning Society." In *New Directions for Adult and Continuing Education*, no. 103: 5–16.

Martin, W. 1986. "Where Is Christian Higher Education Going?" *Faculty Dialogue* 6: 9–26.

Matkin, G. 2004. "Adult Degree Programs: How Money Talks, and What It Tells." In *New Directions for Adult and Continuing Education*, no. 103: 61–71.

McMurtrie, B. 2000. "Future of Religious Colleges Is Bright, Say Scholars and Officials." *Chronicle of Higher Education* 47(8): A41. Accessed June 24, 2012. http://chronicle.com/article/Future-of-Religious-Colleges/10649/.

Merriam, S. 2005. "How Adult Life Transitions Foster Learning and Development." In *New Directions for Adult and Continuing Education*, no. 108: 3–13.

Owens, R. G. 2001. *Organizational Behavior in Education: Instructional Leadership and School Reform*, 7th ed. Needham Heights, MA: Allyn and Bacon.

Pearce, S. 1992. "Survival of Continuing Higher Education; Deans' Perceptions of External Threats." *Journal of Continuing Higher Education* 40(2): 2–7.

Senge, P., and others. 1999. *The Dance of Change: The Challenges of Sustaining Momentum in Learning Organizations*. New York: Currency Doubleday.

Singh, P., and L. Martin. 2004. "Accelerated Degree Programs: Assessing Student Attitudes and Intentions." *Journal of Education for Business* 79(5): 299–305.

Sissel, P., C. Hansman, and C. Kasworm. 2001. "The Politics of Neglect: Adult Learners in Higher Education." In *New Directions for Adult and Continuing Education*, no. 91: 17–28.

Smith, M. 2007. "Administration of Adult Programs: Governance Is Key." In *Systems of Excellence*, edited by S. Drury, 20–28. Marion, IN: Triangle Publishing.

Sparks, P. 1994. "Where Is Nontraditional Education Going? Exploring the Dynamics of Change." *Journal of Continuing Higher Education* 42(1): 23–33.

Terrell, P. 1990. "Adapting Institutions of Higher Education to Serve Adult Students' Needs." *NASPA Journal* 27: 241–247.

Winston, D. 1999. *The Mission, Formation and Diversity Survey Report: Adult Degree Programs at Faith-Based Colleges*. Princeton, NJ: Center for the Study of Religion, Princeton University.

PAMELA A. GILES is an associate professor in the Indiana Wesleyan University School of Nursing, Division of Graduate Studies.

Indiana Wesleyan University enrolls over 3,200 students on its main campus in Marion, Indiana. IWU's decentralized nontraditional programs offer undergraduate and graduate degrees, mostly in business, to over 12,000 students at various sites around the Midwest.

7

Although Bethel University uses separate administrative structures and physical spaces for its three academic units, program planning and student services remain very connected, creating a hybrid balance of centralized and decentralized functions in the overall administrative structure.

Practicing What We Teach: Learning from Experience to Improve Adult Program Administration

Lori K. Jass

Bethel University in St. Paul, Minnesota, comprises three primary units that each serve a distinct population: the College of Arts and Sciences (CAS) is a residential college for roughly 2,800 traditional-age undergraduates; the College of Adult and Professional Studies and Graduate School (CAPS/GS) serves roughly 2,200 adult learners at both the graduate and undergraduate levels; and Bethel Seminary (SEM) provides theological education and ministry training for approximately 1,200 graduate students. The College of Arts and Sciences buildings and the largest of three Seminary campuses are located on a 245-acre wooded, lakeside campus in the Twin Cities metropolitan area. The College of Adult and Professional Studies and Graduate School houses its administrative operations in an office building approximately one-quarter mile from campus and operates classroom buildings in the metro area and out of state.

Bethel University began as Bethel Theological Seminary, later adding a junior college. In 1972, Bethel College and Seminary moved to its current location in Arden Hills, Minnesota. In 1990, the Board of Trustees authorized the creation of the Program in Adult Continuing Education (PACE) to serve adult learners, offering one BA degree completion program in Organizational Studies. PACE grew into the Center for Graduate and Continuing Studies (CGCS) and later became the College of Adult and Professional Studies and Graduate School when the institution became a university. Today CAPS/GS offers an associate of arts degree, bachelor's degrees in seven areas, ten master's degrees, and one doctoral degree.

As CAPS/GS has grown and the institution has changed from a college and seminary to a university, administration of the adult programs has also

New Directions for Higher Education, no. 159, Fall 2012 © Wiley Periodicals, Inc.
Published online in Wiley Online Library (wileyonlinelibrary.com) • DOI:10.1002/he.20027

evolved. A review of our institutional history in relation to the administration of adult programming reveals some organizational structures that have worked well and some that have created distinct challenges. Progress has been uneven in building administrative structures that are optimally supportive of adult programs.

Although many adult learning practitioners argue for complete autonomy for adult programs, Bethel's experience argues for a system that capitalizes on the strengths of centralized services while allowing enough autonomy to enable the adult programs to respond quickly and purposefully to rapidly changing contexts. Put another way, strong adult programs need an opportunity both to *shape* institutional policy and practice and to *be shaped by* institutional policy and practice. This experience is consistent with the conclusion Malcolm Knowles (1980) reached over thirty years ago:

> My observation of adult-education programs in all kinds of institutions across the country supports the generalization that there is a direct correlation between the strength of a program (as measured by size, vitality, quality of output, and support from the system) and its status in the policy-making structure. . . . (However,) the increased power and prestige that come with high organizational status do not in themselves entirely account for improvement in performance . . . the more important consideration is that with autonomy and status the adult-education unit is able to concentrate on processes uniquely effective for the education of adults. (71)

At Bethel, administrative services are generally centralized but include some decentralized elements as well. This structure works best when the vision for and commitment to the adult learner permeates the highest levels of administrative leadership and the adult education unit is free enough to focus on unique processes for adults. To illustrate this, consider the history of two specific administrative and academic support areas: registration and records and academic program management.

Administrative Structure: Registrar's Office

When PACE began, the college leadership hired several staff members to manage the new enterprise. The expectation was that existing administrative units would provide campus services such as registration, financial aid, business office, and so forth. Thus, the registrar's office created the means to manage student enrollment in the new program. As the adult program grew and best practices in adult learning were put into place, the new approach to program delivery taxed the enrollment management system. Existing enrollment structures were not sufficient to handle new demands. Accelerated learning modules required a different management flow. Adult learners' educational histories required new approaches to academic transfer policies. As demands grew, the registrar determined that the adult programs required a dedicated staff member to manage the registration challenges posed by the new unit.

Provided with a dedicated member of the registrar's office staff to serve CAPS/GS, the adult programs were empowered to make adjustments to the system that better fit the needs of the unit. But the customization came at a cost as a chasm began to develop between the new staff member and the traditional registrar's staff, with the CAPS/GS departures from the existing management structure seen as frustrating at best, professionally inappropriate at worst. This tension continued for several years, even as the registrar added additional staff members to attend to the growing needs of CAPS/GS.

When Bethel College became a university, the stage was set for a new way of doing business. Almost simultaneous with the change to university governance, the college's registrar retired and a new campus enterprise management system was researched and selected. Rather than replacing the college registrar, the president asked the seminary registrar to become the first university registrar. One of the first tasks of the university registrar was to be part of a team that would select the new database management system and customize its use for Bethel's future needs. Thus, the new registrar had the opportunity to create a registration and records system that served the diverse needs of three very different student populations and their differing academic formats.

The change in the registrar's office also allowed for a new administrative structure to be put in place. The registrar appointed three associate registrars—one to represent the needs of each academic unit. The associate registrars had dedicated staff to assist them, according to the demands of each unit, in addition to general support staff who assisted all members of the team as needed. This structure is in place today and works well for several reasons. First and foremost, the CAPS/GS associate registrar was chosen based upon the individual's understanding of and commitment to the needs of adult learners. Being an adult student personally, the associate registrar was fully aware of the dynamics that shape an adult learner's ability to succeed and was committed to providing a system that ameliorates the challenges.

The second reason this structure works well is because the current registrar understands the need for *embedded* personnel to handle direct student contact. Though the registrar's office fully handles all back office duties relative to recordkeeping and registration, the direct advising contact with the adult students is handled by program-specific academic advisers who live within the administrative governance of CAPS/GS and have a dotted-line relationship to the registrar's office. Though dotted-line relationships can bring their own challenges, clear communication is facilitated by regular contact and through clear lines of authority and accountability.

The third advantage to this structure is that the back-office demands of the registrar's office that are common to all schools—for example, producing transcripts, processing loan deferments, verifying enrollments, and so forth—are handled by a central staff that can process them more efficiently than individual units could. This speaks to Knowles's (1980) contention that those in the adult education unit should primarily focus their attention on the processes that are uniquely effective for adult learners, and secondarily on systems that provide infrastructural support and are relatively transparent to the learner. Furthermore, the university benefits from economies of scale when purchasing costly supplies like transcript paper, working with the Student Loan Clearinghouse, and providing enrollment verifications and reports.

Finally, the system works well because through regular meetings the registrar and the associate registrar for adult programs continue to invest in understanding the needs of CAPS/GS. The associate registrar is present at CAPS/GS academic meetings to ensure that the registrar's office staff continues to stay abreast of program changes and to ensure that the interests of the registrar's office are brought to bear on academic program changes. Such ongoing engagement is critical to the success of this mainly centralized model because it helps everyone involved in the process stay connected to the rapidly changing needs of adult learners. But, even more important, it ensures that those in the policy-making roles within the institution stay connected to the needs of the adult learner, so their policy making is informed in a broader way to benefit all students.

Academic Structure: Program Development and Management

Just as the relationship between the registrar's office and CAPS/GS has evolved over time, so has the creation and management of academic programs. When PACE began, the academic leaders were members of the CAS faculty who were asked by the administration to serve in this capacity. The first program was developed by customizing a program purchased from an external consultant. Shortly thereafter, nursing and business management programs were developed by existing CAS faculty who agreed—some more enthusiastically than others—to create adult-oriented programs in their disciplines.

Two years after PACE began, there was a marked change in the way programs were developed. At that point, the administrator in charge of the program had a vision for a graduate program to serve a need in the field of education. As a result, the first graduate program was added to the adult unit. Although the program still drew upon the expertise of the established CAS education faculty, it was different in the sense that the vision for the program originated in the adult education unit itself, rather than being requested by central administration.

As new programs continued to be added in subsequent years, some were internally developed adult programs (meaning they grew out of the adult-learning culture of CAPS/GS and were led by faculty who work exclusively for CAPS/GS) and others were externally developed programs that were

NEW DIRECTIONS FOR HIGHER EDUCATION • DOI:10.1002/he

requested by senior university leadership and then birthed from existing CAS departments. As a result, today's programs are a mix of internally developed programs and externally developed programs that are connected to CAS departments. This mix of program models allows for comparison between structures to examine the strengths and weaknesses of each model.

At CAPS/GS, five of the six programs with the highest enrollment were internally developed. They are built upon the theoretical and practical foundation of adult-oriented delivery and instruction, and supported by personnel who are first and foremost adult educators. This seems consistent with Knowles's (1980) observation that "as institutions recognized the unique requirements of serving the educational needs of adults by establishing differentiated administrative units for this purpose, the volume and quality of these services rose dramatically" (71). And though these programs are highly successful in terms of enrollment growth and financial performance, all have been subjected to some criticism by CAS colleagues who consider the programs to be light on rigor and academic quality because of their adult-learning approach.

In comparison, there are several externally developed programs at CAPS/GS that receive consistently positive feedback from CAS colleagues, external accrediting agencies, and the marketplace. These programs have demonstrated extraordinarily high quality over time and have produced highly desirable graduates. These programs have impressed accreditors by developing exceptional assessment plans and ongoing curricular improvement. They have distinguished themselves among competitors by producing graduates who get hired immediately and who are highly recommended to others. But of these half-dozen programs, only one is in the top quartile of programs in terms of enrollment; none are in the top quartile in terms of financial performance. Indeed, these are among the most expensive programs at CAPS/GS—largely due to the fact that they are staffed primarily by full-time faculty whose teaching loads are split between CAS and CAPS/GS.

Based on this summary, one could easily jump to erroneous conclusions: that programs developed on the foundation of the adult-learning model are of lower quality than those that grow out of traditional programs or that programs that grow out of traditional programs cannot be profitable. On the contrary, Bethel's experience suggests that neither of these is automatically true, but rather that a centralized approach to academic program development has the potential to be as helpful as a centralized approach to administrative leadership, if it is managed well.

This conclusion raises the question of what constitutes good management of academic programs. It is clear from Bethel's experience that academic program development and management became more efficient when CAPS/GS gained authority over its academic program decisions. As adult program development continued, program review became increasingly difficult to manage given that approval had to be granted by a committee that was staffed largely by faculty who had no direct knowledge of or experience with CAPS/GS programs or learners. Meetings were held based on CAS calendars, criteria were established based on CAS standards, and evaluation often did not include the criteria most critical to the success of adult programs. However, when CAPS/GS academic affairs committees were instituted to evaluate and approve CAPS/GS programs, some degree of suspicion remained among CAS faculty regarding the ongoing quality of academic programs. Not surprisingly, those programs that enjoyed the most support from CAS colleagues were those that were developed and led by faculty who maintained teaching loads and relationships within both academic units.

It is very important to stress that, contrary to some lingering assumptions, all programs at CAPS/GS were subjected to the same academic evaluation and approval process. In other words, all academic programs were required to demonstrate the same level of quality and rigor as the programs that arose out of CAS departments. It is not accurate to conclude that internally developed programs were substandard in terms of academic quality. And the converse is also true: Those programs that were less financially profitable were still required to meet acceptable financial performance standards.

What is clear is that both sets of programs can improve in ways that are informed by the success of other programs. The externally developed programs are often highly successful from an academic quality perspective largely because they benefit from connection to strong and extensive infrastructural support as part of a CAS department. In the same way that the registrar's office handles back-office duties that free CAPS/GS personnel to focus on adult learners, these departmental infrastructures handle tasks like gathering and processing assessment data, managing complex faculty load issues, and facilitating schedules so their faculty can focus on issues of classroom quality. The challenge for these externally developed programs has been to ensure that the curriculum, which is co-owned by the adult learning unit (CAPS/GS) and the disciplinary department (CAS nursing, education, and so forth), adheres consistently to the values and commitments of adult learning theory.

By contrast, many internally developed programs are highly successful from an enrollment management and fiscal perspective because they were intentionally built upon the foundation of adult learning theory and practice, both from an academic and administrative perspective. They are largely staffed by part-time instructors who are active practitioners in their professional fields, and they are supported by internal staffers who are fully committed to adult learning. Although their academic quality is not in question, their challenge is to ensure that ongoing program evaluation and improvement happens consistently when they do not have the infrastructural support of a fully developed academic department that the externally developed programs enjoy.

This contrast in program models demonstrates the most positive aspect of a centralized administrative model. Done correctly, adult programs can capitalize on the strengths of a differentiated system while simultaneously enjoying the benefits that come with connection to a larger and more comprehensive support structure. But the balancing act is a difficult one. Tipping either direction—which happens more easily than one would imagine—can result in programs that are not true to the requirements of high-quality adult learning or that do not have adequate infrastructural support systems to be healthy and stable.

Learning from Experience: Optimally Effective Management Structures

Bethel University is still working to resolve these tensions. However, successes and failures over the years have helped to identify a few key ingredients that must be present for adult programs to be successful. First and foremost, adult programs need the support and endorsement of leadership at the highest levels of the organization.

> Central to the success of degree programs serving adults is the institutional commitment to the program. This commitment is reflected in the fundamental administrative structure, the financial and budgetary arrangements, the academic systems, and other resource arrangements that support the program. (American Council on Education 1990, 20)

Obviously, it is critical that the governing board authorizes the creation of the adult education unit. But governing boards may have multiple reasons for authorizing the creation of adult education programs—reasons that may or may not include a passion for programs that are built upon sound theory. Therefore, it is most important that institutional leaders—president and provost—thoroughly understand and are passionately committed to the values of adult learning.

Even this commitment, however, is not enough, for it is the policy makers and policy shapers who have the most significant power to impact the success or failure of an adult-learning unit. Peter Senge's (2006) work in learning organizations clearly illustrates the systemic nature of organizations in which changes in one area are not isolated but affect the entire organization. Thus, to be optimally successful, a thorough understanding of the nature of adult learners and a sincere commitment to their success must permeate the policy-shaping leadership of the institution. This understanding and commitment must be in the DNA of all who make policy decisions that affect the institution as a whole. Returning to the example of the registrar's office, the model works only if the registrar stays consciously aware of how any policy decision will impact multiple kinds of students. When institutional policy decisions are made with only one particular constituency in mind, they compromise the other units' ability to succeed because the needs and demands of each constituency are unique even while their systems are interrelated.

Although it is important to ensure that policy makers are imbued with a commitment to the success of adult learners, it is equally important to ensure that those given the responsibility of leadership of adult programs are committed to collegial interaction that ensures their ability to shape policy in helpful ways.

> Administration of an adult college requires a team of faculty with expertise in adult learning theory as well as administrators with operational understanding of how to administer multi-site campuses, recruitment of students and faculty, delivery of resources, and student services. At the same time, such an administrative structure must include people who can converse with traditional academicians and administrators in other parts of the university. (Smith 2007, 21)

Though adult educators nearly uniformly believe that the leader of the adult education unit must have equal status with the leader of the traditional undergraduate unit, representation in senior leadership circles is not enough to ensure that the institution maintains its commitment to adult learning. Rather, "administrators of adult education divisions must understand fully how their parent organization functions if they are to relate to it effectively" (White and Belt 1980, 217). As Senge (2006) asserted, all people bring mental models—beliefs and assumptions—to their work. These assumptions are deeply engrained in all people and can limit their ability to work together because their assumptions limit their ability to engage new perspectives. To more helpfully navigate this potential barrier, those who work primarily with adult programs must be able to do their own cross-cultural communication work. They must be able to identify their own preconceptions, understand the preconceptions of others, and bring light to each in order to deconstruct those that are unhelpful and limiting. In doing so, adult educators can more deftly help shape policies that are supportive of all students.

At Bethel, this critical interpersonal work is compromised by geography. Because the administrative leaders of the adult programs are in an off-campus location, it is more challenging to build and maintain collegial relationships. Not surprisingly, the externally developed programs tend to gain the most consistent support and consideration when policies are formed, largely because the leaders of those programs live both in the traditional college and adult learning unit. Thus, in order to foster the kind of environment that allows for sustained growth and quality of all educational units, "the changes most needed to create a learning infrastructure must take place at the institutional level. . . . (as individuals) have little control over the institutional factors that inhibit creation of alternative learning environments" (Twigg 1994, 4).

It is tempting for adult educators to yearn for the freedom to build internal programs autonomously, to shape their own destiny, and to shake free from what can be experienced as counterproductive connections to traditional educational structures. But adult programs that are fortunate enough to be integrally connected to other kinds of programs may choose instead to embrace the richness that comes with those connections. Much in the same way that adult learners are asked to evaluate and synthesize competing demands into mutually reinforcing structures, leaders of adult programs can come to a place of resolve, leaning into the inherent challenges in order to create new understandings that lead to richer and deeper programs and collegial relationships.

In his work on transformative adult learning, Jack Mezirow (1991) gave an exhortation that is formative for all who work through the challenges of providing strong adult programs in an environment that is not always conducive to maintaining strong connections to adult learning theory:

> We professional adult educators have a commitment to help learners become more imaginative, intuitive, and critically reflective of assumptions; to become more rational through effective participation in critical discourse, and to acquire meaning perspectives that are more inclusive, integrative, discriminating, and open to alternative points of view. By doing this we may help others, and perhaps ourselves, move toward a fuller and more dependable understanding of the meaning of our mutual experience. (224)

May we all, as adult educators, become more imaginative, intuitive, and critically reflective as we seek to become more inclusive, integrative, discriminating, and open to alternative points of view.

References

American Council on Education. 1990. *Principles of Good Practice for Alternative and External Degree Programs for Adults.* Washington, DC: American Council on Education.

Knowles, M. 1980. *The Modern Practice of Adult Education.* Chicago: Follett.

Mezirow, J. 1991. *Transformative Dimensions of Adult Learning.* San Francisco: Jossey-Bass.

Senge, P. 2006. *The Fifth Discipline: The Art and Practice of the Learning Organization.* New York: Doubleday.

Smith, M. A. 2007. "Administration of Adult Programs: Governance Is Key." In *Systems of Excellence,* edited by S. Drury, 20–28. Marion, IN: Triangle Publishing.

Twigg, C. A. 1994. "The Changing Definition of Learning." *Educom Review* 29(4): 4.

White, T., and J. R. Belt. 1980. "Leadership." In *Developing, Administering, and Evaluating Adult Education,* edited by A. B. Knox, 216–248. San Francisco: Jossey-Bass.

LORI K. JASS is the dean of academic affairs for graduate and adult programs at Bethel University in St. Paul, Minnesota.

Bethel University enrolls approximately 6,100 students. The nontraditional programs, first launched in 1991, enroll about 2,200 in over 20 undergraduate and graduate programs.

8

Abilene Christian University uses a hybrid governance model. Centralized structures include traditional program departments that supply the faculty and curriculum development for online graduate programs. Decentralized structures include an associate provost and separate student services for the online program.

Starting from Scratch: The Evolution of One University's Administrative Structure for Adult Programs

Carol G. Williams

Background

In designing its adult online degree program, Abilene Christian University (ACU) faced a number of challenges related in part to its remote location in west Texas and also to the lack of adult program expertise in the university administration. Before the university made major changes in 2004, several units serving adults—the bachelor of applied sciences (BAS), distance education, and continuing education—were parts of the university studies division, a unit, headed by a director, which was not a college but an umbrella unit for programs outside those designed for residential students.

Abilene's only degree-completion program aimed at working adults, the bachelor of applied sciences, struggled to get departments to offer courses at times convenient for adults to attend. There were few night classes and no weekend classes. The main attraction was the half-price tuition these students paid. Distance education consisted of some videoconferenced classes offered for BAS students and a few web courses offered for religion students that were facilitated by the faculty development center. Continuing education was limited to Graduate Record Examinations (GRE) prep courses offered on campus and a few noncredit courses offered through third parties.

In the fall of 2003, a time of budgetary crisis, the university made three significant decisions. First, a strategic planning team recommended the offering of online undergraduate courses during the summer. Two were developed through the professional development center during the spring of 2004 and offered for the first time that summer. Second, the university studies division

New Directions for Higher Education, no. 159, Fall 2012 © Wiley Periodicals, Inc.
Published online in Wiley Online Library (wileyonlinelibrary.com) • DOI:10.1002/he.20028

was disbanded in the fall of 2004. The dean of the graduate school and an associate provost assumed responsibility for distance education, continuing education, and related services. Third, the BAS program was moved to the college of arts and sciences and became a separate department.

In the fall of 2004, the provost convened a university-wide strategic planning committee that was given the task of developing a new vision and rationale for distance education. The committee was made up of the provost, the dean of the graduate school and associate provost, the head of the faculty development center, the director of faculty professional development, the chair of the BAS degree program, the chief information officer, and the chief financial officer.

The committee developed these broad goals:

(1) To use distance education courses to deliver programs currently offered on the ACU campus
(2) To expand ACU's outreach by establishing education centers in key metropolitan areas
(3) To expand ACU's outreach by creating certificate and degree programs delivered entirely online
(4) To expand ACU's outreach through distance continuing education
(5) To expand ACU's outreach through strategic partnerships (Internal report: *Distance Education at Abilene Christian University: Rationale and Goals.* Spring 2005)

Only one member of the committee, the chair of BAS, had a background in adult programs. Also, there were no college deans on the committee. Although the BAS chair advocated for a separate college with a dean, his request went unheeded, and distance education with its adult students and entrepreneurial focus remained under an associate provost who was also the dean of the graduate school and who reported directly to the provost. Therefore, in spite of worthy goals, decisions about the structure of distance education were made without a clear knowledge of their likely consequences and without buy-in from the college deans, a misstep that would become apparent later on.

Through a process of weighting and ranking, the strategic planning committee decided to launch two master's degrees in an online format, one in conflict resolution and one in school leadership. The master's program in conflict resolution and reconciliation was built on an existing fifteen-hour certificate, and the existing master's degree in education for principal certification was completely overhauled. Both degrees were good candidates to move to an online format, because their target audience was working adults, few of whom were likely to move to Abilene.

By the fall of 2005, the university had increased the distance education budget to include extra staff and faculty to begin course development for these online degrees. That fall, the appropriate academic councils approved these online programs. The additional staff included the (former) director of faculty development, who had extensive experience in online programs and who thus headed up course design and delivery, an instructional designer, and an administrative coordinator for a unit temporarily called ACU WorldWide. The additional faculty included one instructor in education and one in conflict resolution. The salaries for these five people were included in the distance education budget, but the faculty were hired and housed by the traditional departments of the college of arts and sciences. The thinking at the time was that these salaries needed to be in the distance education budget so that, should a particular program not succeed or even phase out after some success, the unit would be able to redirect those dollars to some other effort.

A Hybrid System of Governance

Although those leading the efforts did not have the language to express what was being created, they were setting up a hybrid system of governance where faculty and curriculum were in the departments of their traditional colleges, whereas marketing, admissions, and student services were decentralized in a unit headed by the associate provost for distance education. Buy-in from the faculty in those programs as well as from the dean of the college of arts and sciences was high. Because ACU is a relatively small university where everyone knows everyone else, faculty and administrators worked as a team and did not always adhere to strict organizational boundaries or fiefdoms.

In the fall of 2006, ACU WorldWide launched the two master's degrees with an enrollment of 66 students. Course development continued in full swing. The unit, with the support of the provost, began to plan the launch of two or three degree-completion concentrations as well as four more master's degrees for an initial total of six master's degrees. These existing traditional programs would move to online delivery and move away from face-to-face delivery.

The team realized that ACU WorldWide did not have adequate resources, both in money and personnel, to keep up with the anticipated growth. Specifically, the unit did not have the marketing funds and personnel to compete in the online adult arena. Nor was there sufficient technological support at times when adult students would likely be seeking it. BAS programs require a heavy course development load, and the instructional design team assisting faculty members was already pushed to the limit. As a result, ACU WorldWide began to look for companies selling courses that could be imbued with the university's faith-based worldview.

In August of 2007, after a period of intense evaluation, the university signed a contract with a leading provider of online learning services to do marketing, admissions, student services, hosting, and technical support twenty-four hours a day, seven days a week. That fall, ACU WorldWide enrolled 124 students in the existing programs and later transferred student data to the provider's servers and support structures. In March 2008, ACU WorldWide, which was renamed ACU Online, launched four new master's degrees. All six master's degrees shared some courses.

Meanwhile the university increased the unit's budget to allow for hiring additional faculty and support staff. Although the outside service provider was taking on many responsibilities, ACU Online still needed additional personnel in financial aid in addition to instructors in the education and conflict resolution departments. Again, these salary lines were kept in the distance education budget, although the hiring and evaluation were done by the college or support service unit.

By the fall of 2010, the online programs had grown to 460 students in five master's degrees (the sixth master's degree had been merged with one of the other degrees) and four graduate certificates.

ACU Online Today

Currently, the five online master's degrees and four graduate certificates designed for adult students are administered through ACU Online, a unit headed by the associate provost for online programs. Student support services, as well as marketing and admissions, are decentralized. Faculty and curriculum development, however, are centralized in their respective departments and colleges. This chapter presents the advantages and disadvantages of such a hybrid system while addressing the challenges that lie ahead as the university looks for the best structure to increase enrollment of adult students.

Currently, ACU Online's budget consists of 4.5 faculty FTEs, 3.5 staff FTEs housed in other areas, and 6 instructional designers and office personnel. For the past two fiscal years, ACU Online has covered its budget and returned a surplus to the university. Student enrollment in ACU Online is growing faster than in any other area of the university. Looking from the outside, one might surmise that the current organizational structure is serving the university well.

But there are challenges. ACU Online is headed by the associate provost for online programs. She reports directly to the provost and no longer also serves as graduate dean. ACU Online manages the partnership with the provider, aids faculty in developing courses, and supervises the interaction between the provider and the ACU personnel with whom they interface. Essentially, all support services are decentralized within ACU Online. The ACU Online budget includes several faculty and staff lines that report to other units, and ACU Online has its own revenue expectation.

Full-time ACU Online faculty members reside in the departments of their respective colleges (two different colleges at this time). The faculty are hired and evaluated by their college departments and dean, although it is ACU Online that protects the faculty lines. Departments and deans are also responsible for the curriculum covered in the degrees. ACU Online cannot create an online program without the consent and approval of the faculty and deans in the traditional colleges. Thus, even though there may be a campus program that would serve an adult audience well, the faculty along with the dean of the particular college must approve the program for online delivery. The associate provost's only power in arranging for new programs is one of persuasion.

Evaluating the Structure

What are the advantages and disadvantages of ACU's structure—a centralized curriculum and faculty and decentralized support services?

An important advantage is that distance education faculty members are integrated with traditional faculty members in their colleges and are available to refute any notions that online courses are of inferior quality or that they lack the sense of community that characterizes face-to-face courses. Distance faculty members often make presentations about their courses at faculty development luncheons, allowing traditional faculty to see into the world of online learning.

A second advantage is that by anchoring each of the programs with faculty members who have offices on campus, who go through the usual tenure and promotion process, and who participate in campus committees, the online programs are more clearly seen as part of the university than if they were housed in a separate unit. Although this is a positive factor, it has also led some members of the university community to think of ACU Online programs as regular graduate programs simply delivered online, rather than as programs uniquely aimed at the adult education market.

Student services staff members who are dedicated to adult students represent another advantage. Because the online programs run on an entirely different delivery schedule from the residential campus and because the campus as a whole is focused on the undergraduate residential student, it would be difficult to train the existing campus support personnel to respond well to this adult audience.

A final advantage is that the marketing and admissions team from the outside service provider deals well with adults and uses an economy of scale for purchasing media. Although an ACU representative reviews and approves all marketing materials and all scripts used by admissions personnel, having these functions performed by a specialized unit frees ACU Online from having to "wait in line" behind those requesting such services for residential students on campus.

One of the big disadvantages is that ACU Online's ability to earn revenue is limited by its dependence on the departments to develop (or simply approve) programs for delivery to adults. At this point, the graduate programs most likely to be viable in an online form, with both faculty buy-in and marketing, are already available. Seeking new programs or attempting to modify existing campus programs for online delivery is now a matter of persuasion on the part of the associate provost for online programs. There are many other campus activities and programs at ACU—the mobile learning initiative and the new core curriculum to name two—that compete for the time and attention of deans and departments.

Another disadvantage with this system is that there is a tendency on the part of the departments to want to design faculty workloads in more traditional ways. This again cuts into the net revenue of ACU Online. ACU made a commitment to use a few full-time faculty in each program to ensure quality; however, ACU Online does employ a model of delivery (one lead teacher with small-group facilitators leading sections) that provides a more economical way to deploy faculty. Sometimes deans still write nine-month contracts for the ACU Online faculty even though their workload spreads over twelve months with nontraditional breaks. Continuing to put these faculty members on tenure track also lessens the flexibility of ACU Online to deploy these faculty resources efficiently.

The faculty in ACU Online might say that the biggest disadvantage to this system is that they feel they have two deans; faculty are not sure who controls which activities and to whom they should report. The associate provost holds biweekly meetings for the directors of online programs and occasional meetings for the faculty as well. Online faculty members from various departments benefit from meeting together because, despite the fact they teach different subjects, they share many of the same challenges—challenges that are often quite different from those faced by faculty members who teach only residential students.

A final disadvantage is that there can often be gaps in communication between the various campus units that must interact on behalf of adults—financial aid, registrar, and so forth—and the various adult student services. Fortunately, ACU has personnel in key positions who can adjust the student information system in order to accommodate the nontraditional student population.

As mentioned earlier, hindsight suggests the error of not putting college deans on the original strategic planning team. Because the deans ultimately control the faculty and programs in their colleges, their lack of buy-in and ownership hinders ACU Online's ability to offer new programs.

The outsourcing partnership with the external provider has generally been a positive one. By contracting with this service, ACU was able to move quickly into the online marketplace. Because the provider makes the majority of the upfront investments, ACU was able to get the programs up and running much more quickly than if it had had to build the campus infrastructure itself. Because ACU did not have a strong adult unit on which to build and because it is located in a rural area, the decision to outsource was definitely a good one. However, there has been some suspicion around campus that the provider has too much control and is demanding too large a portion of the tuition revenue. Despite efforts to affirm that ACU holds total control of curriculum, courses, and faculty and that ACU approves all marketing and admissions efforts, that perception has no doubt hurt ACU Online's ability to secure cooperation from some areas of the university and thus to attract new programs.

ACU Online now stands at a crossroads. By many standards, the venture into online education has been quite successful with the existing organizational structure. Enrollment has grown to 460 students in four years, and degree offerings have grown from two master's degrees to five master's degrees and four graduate certificates. For two years now, ACU Online has returned net revenue to the university. At this time, enrollment growth seems to be leveling off, and there are no new programs to be launched in the near term. The university administration wishes to expand the programs and the enrollment, but will the current organizational structure permit that? Has the organizational structure that gave birth to distance education at ACU become untenable? Is there a better one for ACU's future? These are the questions with which the university now wrestles.

CAROL G. WILLIAMS *is a professor emeritus of mathematics and former associate provost for online programs at Abilene Christian University.*

Abilene Christian University is located in Abilene, Texas, and enrolls 4,700 students. The online graduate degree programs designed for adult learners enroll over 500 students.

NEW DIRECTIONS FOR HIGHER EDUCATION • DOI:10.1002/he

9

Eastern Mennonite University's adult program uses a hybrid governance structure. Functions separated from the traditional program include marketing, admissions, and student advising. Functions that remain connected to the traditional program include the registrar, financial aid, and student business accounts.

Hybrid Governance in an Adult Program: A Nuanced Relationship

Suzanne Cockley

Introduction

One of the unique characteristics of small liberal arts colleges is the rich sense of tradition carried through the years, handed down from one graduating class to the next. Most small institutions have idiosyncratic traditions based on quasi myths, and the fact that these are as dear to the heart of the most senior professor as they are to the young freshman at midyear is a particularly special aspect of the small-college working environment. The perennial challenge, though, is to discern when a traditional way of doing things is worth keeping despite the costs and when it has lost much of its original meaning and should be put aside.

In the case of nontraditional degree completion programs, one important strategy in this discernment is the deliberate separation of academic rigor and curricular design from delivery logistics and institutional operations. How do we maintain the quality that makes a degree from our institution meaningful and valuable while being willing to do business in a very different way? At Eastern Mennonite University (EMU), we manage this by adopting a hybrid model, choosing a traditional approach for some aspects of our program and developing a variety of more contemporary options for others. This is more a process guided by principles than a decision made years ago and set in place—it is ongoing and requires a deliberate return to our principles each time a new issue arises.

A degree completion program at EMU was first discussed in the late 1980s. Administrators were aware that many small colleges were adopting specialized programs to attract working adults who had some college experience

New Directions for Higher Education, no. 159, Fall 2012 © Wiley Periodicals, Inc.
Published online in Wiley Online Library (wileyonlinelibrary.com) • DOI:10.1002/he.20029

but had left college before earning a diploma. The most striking feature of these programs was their ability to generate money for the institution. Normally this would have been enough to cause EMU administrators to dismiss the idea, fearing that these programs sacrificed academics in favor of a quick profit. However, when these programs began to appear at our peer institutions, especially when a sister Mennonite college launched an adult degree completion program, EMU administrators took a second look.

As the discussion was brought to larger institutional audiences, particularly the undergraduate faculty, concerns were raised about the academic quality of these programs and whether or not it would be possible to incorporate certain EMU distinctive characteristics, namely our emphasis on cross-cultural learning and our Anabaptist Christian perspective. In addition to these curriculum questions, the faculty was concerned about the application of prior life learning toward earning college credit, a practice common in many adult degree completion programs. On the other hand, the introduction of a completely new population of students to the campus was regarded as an exciting development for the EMU community and mission.

When those charged with investigating degree completion programs discovered the adult program at Spring Arbor College, many of the concerns were put to rest, at least for the moment. EMU purchased the Spring Arbor curriculum for a management and organizational development major in 1993. The program included detailed suggestions for setting up the logistics of the program in our existing business structure, as well as enough flexibility in the curriculum to insert two courses that we created to address cross-cultural learning and Anabaptist Christian perspectives. While these adjustments were being made, the college community's attention turned to an even larger discussion around the addition of graduate programs and the possibility of moving to university status. In the shadow of this larger debate, the Adult Degree Completion Program (ADCP) started in 1995 with seventeen students, a small staff, and relatively little fanfare.

In the years since, EMU has added a second major in nursing to the program and a second location in Lancaster, Pennsylvania. We have revised the curriculum and tweaked policies regarding payment and financial aid. We also have made changes to stay in line with the rest of the institution as it updated technology and revised general education requirements. The program has grown so that currently more than 25 percent of the baccalaureate graduates at each annual commencement are ADCP students. At the present time, 94 percent of ADCP students finish the program. In general, the program has been fairly stable and consistently meets the requirements of the Southern Association of Colleges and Schools, our regional accreditation body. The financial benefits of the program have become a very important part of the university budget, and strong interest of local community members in the program indicates that it fills an important need.

NEW DIRECTIONS FOR HIGHER EDUCATION • DOI:10.1002/he

Program Description

ADCP at EMU is an upper-division cohort-based program. A cohort of twenty students begins four times each calendar year. Students must have already earned sixty semester hours of credit and have had significant previous work experience. We rarely accept students under twenty-five years of age.

We are currently beginning two management cohorts and two nursing cohorts each year at the main campus location and three nursing cohorts at the Lancaster, Pennsylvania, location. A cohort generally meets one evening each week for four hours, although the Lancaster program regularly offers a daytime cohort for nurses. The students in the cohort take one course at a time. A three-semester-hour course usually meets for five weeks. The order of the courses is set, and the students in the cohort go through all the courses as a group. The program runs year round, with the management program lasting sixteen months and the nursing program eighteen months. We emphasize the benefits of the cohort as a learning community and offer the program only on site.

The management and nursing programs cover courses in the major. ADCP students also must meet general education requirements, which are slightly different from the requirements for traditional undergraduates, but generally congruent. For students who lack general education credits, we offer several general education evening courses throughout the year. Alternatively, students can take general education and elective courses at other colleges or universities, or they can follow a detailed portfolio procedure for earning credit for life learning or other types of informal learning.

ADCP courses are taught by a combination of full-time instructors who teach exclusively for ADCP, full-time instructors who teach primarily in the traditional program, and adjuncts—particularly individuals with significant work experience in their fields.

ADCP's Place in the University

The ADCP director reports to the provost. Although the ADCP curriculum is clearly an undergraduate program, the student population has much more in common with graduate students. As a result ADCP does not fit completely in either the undergraduate or graduate programs.

The ways in which ADCP relates to the rest of the university exemplify a combination of the traditional and the new, as discussed previously. The ADCP adheres to the following guiding principles: (1) maintain a high-quality academic program that emphasizes EMU's core values and provides students with a significant learning experience; (2) demonstrate a clear focus on learning that builds on and enhances the work life of students; and (3) to the extent possible within our core values and fiscal realities, remove obstacles to college enrollment for working adults.

NEW DIRECTIONS FOR HIGHER EDUCATION • DOI:10.1002/he

Almost every relationship between ADCP and other university entities is mediated by all three principles, but the first principle is most apparent in the relationship between ADCP and the traditional undergraduate faculty. The second principle is most evident in the particular policies and practices of ADCP, and the third principle guides our connection with university offices.

Connections with University Offices

The adult program at Eastern Mennonite University connects with the central administrative functions at varying levels of autonomy.

Marketing. ADCP plans for, arranges, evaluates, and pays for its own marketing and advertising activities. In recent years the university marketing office has focused on a uniform logo and messaging, and this has meant that the ADCP staff person in charge of marketing works more closely with the university marketing office to gain approval for our efforts. However, most of the legwork is still done by an ADCP staff member who also keeps the ADCP section of the university website up to date. The Lancaster program has a separate marketing person as well as a separate budget.

Admissions. Potential students responding to advertisements contact the ADCP office directly. We create and distribute printed program material. We meet with potential students and support them throughout the admissions process. The university admissions office has no involvement with ADCP admissions. ADCP has its own admissions committee, which is made up of the adult program directors at both sites and a full-time faculty member from both the traditional business and traditional nursing departments. During the admissions process, the ADCP office works with the registrar to evaluate student transcripts and develop a rating sheet that documents which courses are transferred to EMU and which graduation requirements remain to be completed.

The ADCP office enters new students into the data management system. The university information technology department assigns an ID number and computer log-in. When a cohort is assembled and begins classes, the ADCP office sends the enrollment information to the registrar's office where the entire cohort is enrolled in each course of the program.

Registrar. The relationship with the registrar's office is governed by both the first and third principles. We depend on the registrar to make judgments about transferred courses based on how he makes those decisions for transfer students entering the traditional program. On the other hand, we do depart in several ways from some traditional registrar policies in order to meet the needs of adult students completing college degrees that were begun many years ago.

Student Advising and Student Life. ADCP covers all student advising for the program. Faculty advisers meet with students before the program to explain exactly what courses they will need to graduate. Student advising happens formally on several occasions throughout the program and after the student finishes the major program, as well as informally on numerous occasions. The director monitors and works directly with academically at-risk students in the program. ADCP students are eligible for student life services; however, except for career counseling, they rarely take advantage of these services.

Business Office and Financial Assistance Office. The relationship between the ADCP and the business and financial aid offices most clearly draws on the third principle. Both of these offices manage accounts for ADCP students and process student loan paperwork. ADCP policies follow policies for traditional students to a limited extent. For example, ADCP students who are receiving tuition reimbursement from their employers are exempt from finance charges for a set period of time in order to accommodate the requirement most employers have for grade reports before reimbursement. Regarding financial aid, ADCP students are not eligible for the state tuition assistance grant (TAG) or for other EMU financial aid programs offered to traditional students. They are eligible for government student loan programs and Pell grants, and the university financial aid office manages these programs for ADCP students.

The ADCP has much more involvement with student business affairs than does a traditional academic department. With the traditional program, student enrollment, posting of tuition fees, and application for financial aid happen on a predictable schedule, often linked to the beginning of fall and spring semesters. The ADCP enrolls new students four times a year. With up to six cohorts attending year round on their own schedules, enrollment, grades, and tuition payments are processed almost continuously. The ACDP office works with the business and financial aid offices to bear some of this burden. For example, we directly monitor student accounts and communicate with students who are behind on loan paperwork or payments.

In essence, most of the special policies ADCP uses to make college attendance more realistic for working adults cause more work for the university registrar, business office, and financial assistance office. We are able to maintain these more favorable policies in part by assisting the university's support offices.

Connections with the Traditional Undergraduate Faculty

There are several points of formal connection between ADCP and the undergraduate faculty. These are in place in order to maintain academic quality in the ADCP curriculum. When a new instructor is hired to teach any ADCP course, the individual must be approved by the appropriate academic department to teach that particular course. Likewise, when a new ADCP course is developed or undergoes a major revision, the appropriate academic department must approve it. In this way, an academic department has a significant measure of control over the course offerings that would normally be associated with that department's academic territory. By reviewing and approving the curriculum, traditional faculty are able to judge for themselves if the course is appropriately rigorous, if the scope and depth of the content is appropriate for an undergraduate course, and if the assessment methods are adequate.

Faculty from the business and nursing departments are represented on both the ADCP admissions and assessment committees. The latter group reviews applications for credit for life learning by way of a very detailed and standardized portfolio process. This process was developed when the ADCP began and was reviewed and approved by the entire undergraduate faculty. This was done out of recognition that credit for nonformal learning was a particular concern. The undergraduate faculty members who serve on these two committees are appointed by the provost. They may have experience with ADCP instruction, but that is not a requirement.

Finally, as ACDP director, I have put thought and effort into relating to the traditional faculty through teaching and university committee service. I teach three courses twice a year in the ADCP management program not only to get to know our students better but also to be able to speak with true knowledge about the program and our students when concerns are raised about quality or the need for particular policies. In addition I have taught a graduate course in EMU's master's in education program for several years, and I regularly attend faculty meetings. I have served on university committees as chair of the institutional review board, on faculty hiring and contract review committees, on an instructional technology planning committee, and on a special task force to review the structure of the institution. I have collaborated with the chair of the nursing department to develop a master's in nursing program using some of the structure of ADCP as a model, and I have audited courses taught by my colleagues both for my own benefit and to support fellow instructors.

Benefits of the Hybrid Model

We attribute our growing enrollment and strong retention and graduation rates to the cohort model, our high staff-to-student ratio, and the day-to-day flexibility that is a result of our particular hybrid administrative model.

By doing a lot of the work related to communicating with students and monitoring financial matters and enrollment, we retain a high degree of control over the program and its policies. There are regular calls for ADCP to be more like the traditional program. Although it is important to take these requests seriously, especially when we can modify the program to make life easier for support offices, it is also crucial that we keep enough control over policies and procedures to ensure the program remains a realistic educational opportunity for working adults.

Maintaining close ties with academic departments and involving non-ADCP faculty as much as possible in portfolio assessment, ADCP committees, and hiring of instructors keeps the program solid and helps the rest of the university feel confident of its quality. Frequent interaction with the traditional faculty often produces good suggestions for improving the program.

Challenges of the Hybrid Model

Such a nuanced relationship requires constant monitoring. Because the external environment and the university environment are always changing, we must return again and again to our core principles to make decisions. After 15 years, some of the ADCP ways of doing things have become stale and lifeless traditions, and we find it is time to let them go. For example, we have greatly streamlined the convocation at the beginning of each cohort. On the other hand, as our non-Mennonite students began asking more questions about the Mennonite faith, we added a session to the bible course when our university president (who is also ordained) visits the class and gives candid answers to their questions. The program is flexible enough to make these necessary adjustments.

As ADCP enrollment grows, the burdens we place on university support offices become greater. It is not always possible for our staff to take on significant tasks to relieve the support offices. For example, a recent change in database programs has made access to certain financial information unavailable to our staff, resulting in less ability to monitor student accounts and communicate with students who are falling behind in payments.

It is reasonable to say that almost everyone at EMU knows about ADCP and recognizes it as a crucial component to the life of the community because of its financial contributions to the institution but also because it is a program that fills a significant need in our larger community. However, there are still times when the program's quality is questioned and evidence must be shown to support its continuation. The fact that ADCP is so profitable is a very mixed blessing. We are recognized as indispensable, but not always embraced as a fundamental part of EMU that is crucial to institutional identity and mission, not just to the institutional balance sheet.

Mutually Beneficial Relationships Between Adult Degree Programs and the Liberal Arts

The Association of American Colleges and Universities (n.d.) offers a clear and useful definition of liberal education:

> Liberal education is an approach to learning that empowers individuals and prepares them to deal with complexity, diversity, and change. It provides students with broad knowledge of the wider world as well as in-depth study in a specific area of interest. A liberal education helps students develop a sense of social responsibility, as well as strong and transferable intellectual and practical skills such as communication, analytical and problem-solving skills, and a demonstrated ability to apply knowledge and skills in real-world settings.

When a college educator working with traditional students reads this definition, a picture of standard courses—for example, introductory courses in art history, sociology, and biology—come to mind, plus a few specialized courses like a senior seminar that aims at drawing many concepts together. Perhaps interdisciplinary courses are used to develop the ability to transfer learning. Community learning or study-abroad programs can enhance the ability to apply knowledge in real-world setting. But when adult program educators see this definition, they will see immediately how well most adult programs match this description, particularly in the specific items that relate learning to real-life and practical communication skills.

Liberal education emphasizes both grand themes and practical application. Because the ADCP curriculum is preplanned and consistent, themes are easily incorporated into many different courses and can be developed over time. The traditional program at EMU has identified these themes in our core values, and we strive to build them into our curricula so that every student is exposed to them.

The ADCP curriculum emphasizes the use of students' work experience as a springboard for academic learning, focusing on praxis—the interplay between theory and practice. Although practical application is often theoretical and delayed for traditional students, it is real and immediate for ADCP students.

These aspects of the ADCP structure and curriculum make it an interesting model of an alternative way of providing liberal education. Traditional and ADCP perspectives are very compatible, and the potential for learning from each other is great. The traditional program can use ADCP curriculum examples to help build conceptual themes throughout the four-year program. The traditional program can also find ways to be more deliberate about understanding the experiences young students bring to campus and using them as learning platforms.

Finally, the nature of ADCP has led EMU into a better relationship with many people in the local community. The structure of ADCP means that most of our students live within a one-hour commute of campus. Therefore, the student population is very local and very non-Mennonite, compared to the traditional student population. As ADCP students learn about EMU and, more indirectly, about Mennonites, they take their new understandings back into the surrounding community. For many local residents, Mennonites seem to be a closed community, people who choose to isolate themselves socially and economically. Our ADCP students are helping to dispel this image, and in return we Mennonites at EMU have a new appreciation for how many non-Mennonites hold values similar to ours.

Of course, the benefits move in the other direction as well. A campus-based program shares the environment of the traditional program—ADCP students say they are getting an authentic college learning experience simply because they come to a beautiful campus for classes. The annual commencement is a very moving event for ADCP students, who participate along with the traditional students. These particular traditions of higher education are very meaningful for adult students.

EMU's solid academic reputation in our local community, especially for our nursing program, greatly enhances the image of ADCP. We have tried to choose majors that are able to build on the strengths of the traditional academic programs. Traditional undergraduate faculty have helped us orient many of our courses in particularly helpful ways, due to their experience teaching and practicing.

Conclusion

EMU's hybrid administrative model is certainly a work in progress. Over fifteen years the program has experienced slow changes as people have come and gone, glitches have arisen, and fixes have been implemented. Recent economic conditions have had their effect on adult enrollment and the ability of students to afford the program. Whereas our first students had only basic experience with technology, today's adult students demand instructional technology and present some of the same classroom dilemmas with cell phones and social media, such as Facebook, as do younger students. We have not realized all the possible benefits of this structure, nor have we solved all the problems. It is clear that neither traditional programs nor nontraditional programs can afford to ignore calls for change, but it is critical that administrators of both programs maintain a clear vision of what is important to the mission of the whole institution. This can be accomplished only through mutual appreciation and collaboration.

References

Association of American Colleges and Universities. n.d. *What Is Liberal Education?* http://www.aacu.org/leap/what_is_liberal_education.cfm.

Association of American Colleges and Universities. n.d. *What Is a 21st Century Liberal Education?* Accessed June 24, 2012. http://www.aacu.org/leap/what_is_liberal_education.cfm.

SUZANNE COCKLEY *is the director of the adult degree completion program at Eastern Mennonite University in Harrisonburg, Virginia.*

Eastern Mennonite University enrolls over 1,500 students. The nontraditional program offers degrees in business and nursing to over 200 students.

10

Stephen D. Holtrop defines the assumptions going into this study, reviews patterns in the case studies, and describes results of a follow-up survey on adult programs.

Conclusion: Unique Adult Degree Programs with Unique Relationships to the Main Campus

Stephen D. Holtrop

The chapters in this volume, in addition to the follow-up survey described in this chapter, constitute a study of the way adult education programs in small private colleges and universities relate to the institutions of which they are a part. The chapters not only present many variations of organizational relationships but also reveal some common themes that this concluding chapter will explore.

The editors and many of the authors of this collection of case studies assumed going into this study that the administrative structures of adult programs could be arranged on a single continuum between the extremes of total centralization to total autonomy of functions. That is, we expected that we would see a range of institutions on a continuum between (a) all or almost all adult program functions being shared with the traditional program's functions on the main campus and (b) adult programs with their own entirely separate functions such as admissions, financial aid, advising, curriculum design, and even fund-raising. Further, we assumed that we would find each institution moving in the same direction, albeit at its own pace, along the continuum—namely, away from centralization of control and toward greater autonomy for the adult program. In fact, the planned purpose of the study was to help institutions first situate themselves on the perceived continuum and then conceptualize the process of moving from centralized to autonomous adult programs.

These assumptions were not accurate. Instead we found that institutions vary widely in terms of administrative structures, and each institution represents a unique set of circumstances. Some institutions are moving

NEW DIRECTIONS FOR HIGHER EDUCATION, no. 159, Fall 2012 © Wiley Periodicals, Inc.
Published online in Wiley Online Library (wileyonlinelibrary.com) • DOI:10.1002/he.20030

toward less centralization, although the examples of this seem to focus on autonomy for specific administrative structures in the adult program. Some institutions have moved back toward centralization of almost all functions, physically bringing their off-campus adult programs onto the main campus and reintegrating administrative functions with those of the traditional undergraduate or graduate programs. Some institutions have moved toward hybrid structures while developing more or less centralization, whereas others are staying with a balance of centralized and distributed functions they have found to be effective.

Case Study Interpretations

Two case studies, Eastern University and Alaska Pacific University, illustrate unexpected direction of movement. These previously decentralized institutions have moved their nontraditional operations back onto the main campus, garnering unanticipated faculty understanding and greater buy-in for the adult program than they had experienced before. Although staffing costs and unique geographic contexts drove these changes, an unintended result was an increase in faculty buy-in that also seemed to raise academic quality.

The case study featuring Lipscomb University, however, demonstrates the expected desire on the part of adult program staff to move toward a more distributed, decentralized model. The author of this case study describes challenges experienced when adult programs must share almost all of their functions with the traditional program.

Toward the other end of the continuum, the most distributed or decentralized programs in our collection also represent different patterns of sharing administrative functions with the main campus. North Park University's adult program has its own full-time faculty and academic governance but shares recruiting, financial aid, student accounts, and career services with the traditional program. Indiana Wesleyan University (IWU) started its adult programs in the 1980s and moved steadily toward autonomous decentralized governance models. Having also outgrown its corporate partner, IWU now has fairly autonomous adult program campuses in multiple states, but curriculum development and student accounts remain centralized.

Our examples of hybrid governance models also demonstrate interesting differences. The three case studies in this category again represent different institutions in different geographical locations and with different institutional priorities. Bethel University uses separate administrative structures and physical locations around St. Paul, Minnesota, for its adult programs, but program planning and student services remain very connected to the main campus. Bethel emphasizes institutional unity of mission in all programs while giving individual programs freedom and resources to operate uniquely. By contrast, Abilene Christian University (ACU) has separate student services to address the needs of its online program but shares faculty and curriculum development between its traditional and adult programs. An outside partner provides marketing, admissions, and technology support for the ACU Online program. Representing yet another combination, Eastern Mennonite University's (EMU's) adult program provides its own marketing, admissions, and student advising, while remaining coupled to the traditional program's registrar, financial aid, and student accounts services. Traditional undergraduate academic departments approve all courses in the adult program at EMU.

Author Survey

A follow-up survey of the chapter authors showed that most see their institutions operating with a balance between centralized and decentralized governance functions—that is, some kind of combination of shared and autonomous functions. Regardless of the institutional governance category identified for this study (centralized, distributed, or hybrid), most authors saw their institutions closer to the middle ground ("fairly balanced between centralized and decentralized governance functions"). Interestingly, the chapter authors' predictions for their institutions two years from now were that there would be little movement from the current structures even if the authors' sense of the ideal would be to nudge their programs toward more autonomy.

Authors representing programs in the centralized category saw their institutions on the centralized part of our scale, to be sure, but they were not grouped at the extreme ("very centralized"). Similarly, authors representing the distributed or decentralized category in general also tended to see their institutions closer to the center than the extreme. Predictably, the authors representing a hybrid structure also grouped their responses close to the center, although one such author predicted an institutional shift toward a very centralized model.

Additional Survey

Because of the small number of case study authors represented in each category in this volume, we decided to send a similar survey to several listservs with members representing private colleges and universities with adult programs. These listservs are sponsored by the Christian Adult Higher Education Association (CAHEA), the Association of Christian Distance Education (ACCESS), and the Center for Research in Adult Learning (CRAL), hosted by Indiana Wesleyan University and the Council for Christian Colleges and Universities (CCCU). The results of this survey are discussed next and provide a broader statistical context for the case studies in this volume.

Members of the three listservs received questions in April 2011 about their adult programs. The surveys asked respondents to make judgments about their current governance structures for adult programs, to make a prediction about any future movement toward or away from decentralization, and to indicate which of twenty administrative functions are currently decentralized.

Thirty-three people responded to the survey including thirteen deans or vice presidents of adult programs, eleven directors of adult programs, five adult program faculty or staff members, two deans or chairs of a division of business, one president of a university, and one president of a company that provides educational services to adult programs.

Concerning their perception of their current situation, one-third of the respondents saw their adult program functions as centralized. Slightly more (39 percent) saw their adult programs as decentralized. Almost a quarter saw centralized and decentralized functions being fairly balanced at their institutions. However, central campus administrators tended to see their institutions as more centralized than respondents who worked in adult programs only.

As a group the survey respondents saw the ideal for their institution as somewhat more decentralized than their perception of the current situation. Only five respondents indicated that their ideal structure would be more centralized than their current situation. These five represented all levels of administration at their institutions.

When asked to predict their institutional model for governance of adult education in two years, respondents predicted a move toward either more centralized or more decentralized structures with few seeing a balance of the two. Seven respondents predicted their institutions would be more centralized in two years. Five saw more decentralization in two years. Responses on this item did not seem to correlate with different levels of administration.

During the course of this project, it became clear that institutions create widely varying models of administrative functioning. Among the more decentralized institutions, for example, there was variety among the particular administrative functions that were decentralized. Our follow-up survey sought to find trends and similarities among institutions by listing twenty administrative functions and asking respondents to identify which functions are decentralized or autonomous for their adult programs. The following functions were listed in the survey and are arranged here according to the number of respondents reporting the function as decentralized or autonomous. Respondents listing significantly fewer than ten autonomous functions tended to represent the smallest institutions in this sample.

New Directions for Higher Education • DOI:10.1002/he

Decentralized/Autonomous Services

Advising	85%
Recruiting	79%
Program development	76%
Admissions	73%
Marketing	70%
Curriculum development	70%
Faculty training	67%
Market research	61%
Academic support services	55%
Budgeting	55%
Spiritual development	52%
Academic dean or VP	52%
Academic committee or governance council	42%
Personal counseling	33%
Financial aid	30%
Bookstore	30%
Registrar	24%
Career services	21%
Student business accounts (e.g., billing)	21%
Technology services	12%

Among the thirteen respondents who rated their institutions as mostly or very decentralized, more administrative functions, predictably, were decentralized or autonomous for their adult programs. The ranking of that group's list was similar to the ranking in the table, indicating a consistent sequence in decentralizing administrative functions.

Regardless of the overall institutional model for the adult program, advising and recruiting are likely to be separate (distributed) functions at a majority of institutions. Functions such as curriculum development and faculty training are also very likely to be separate functions. However, separate financial aid and registrar functions for the adult programs are unlikely at most of the institutions surveyed. These functions are more likely to become separate as the adult program grows or the institution moves toward a more decentralized structure overall. According to these survey data, some of the last functions to be separated from the central campus would be the bookstore, career services, technology services, and student billing.

Final Observations

So what advice do we have for administrators in adult programs—especially if they may be frustrated with feeling like the forgotten stepchild on campus? We hope the data presented here in conjunction with the case studies throughout this volume can help give some direction and sense of solidarity with others in similar situations. Additionally, we think the following conclusions are warranted.

First, this study focuses on administrative structures. It is not specifically a study of academic quality issues, fiscal strategy, campus communication, effective staffing, or internal politics. Nonetheless, the case studies presented here deal with these issues as well. The campus ethos presented in these chapters may spark a sense that others share the reader's concerns. Examination of the different administrative models and the concomitant campus dynamics may help to spur changes on the reader's campus, and the ranking of administrative structures in the survey results may help readers decide how to prioritize changes on their own campuses.

Second, the results of this study indicate the need to consider more than simply the autonomy of the adult program's administrative functions. Institutions are considering cost-effectiveness in every decision. Traditional program faculty and administrators often have a role in the adult program, if only in program approval. Internal public relations and faculty buy-in are crucial to many adult program administrators since faculty members are so important in the quality and mission-fit of an adult program. So it may be much more important to increase traditional faculty members' involvement in an adult program than to worry about separating adult program billing processes from the main campus business office.

Third, every institution is different. The adult program at Alaska Pacific University had the type of autonomy that many authors of our volume would envy, but severe cuts in federal funding for education in remote areas forced the institution to recombine functions with the main campus. Similarly, Eastern University brought its adult program on campus when a new building was built to house the various community outreach programs. In both cases, an unexpected but very useful result was more faculty buy-in for the adult program. Even very decentralized and mature adult programs—for example, at North Park and Indiana Wesleyan—share some key functions with their traditional programs. Each institution must weigh the pros and cons of autonomy in each of the administrative areas and avoid sacrificing unity of vision and purpose across the institution.

Fourth, despite the wide variety of approaches represented in the case studies and survey data, there are some clear similarities. Generally, adult program administrators crave more autonomy than they currently have. And generally as adult programs grow, institutions find it necessary to separate adult functions from those that serve traditional-age students. The case studies provide different scenarios with different combinations of decentralized functions, whereas the survey data provide a ranking of administrative functions in the order in which most institutions seem to decentralize them.

We hope that readers will identify with one or two case studies and compare their administrative models to the ranking of the functions. In this way the volume may provide pointers for strategically planning an adult program's next steps for building additional capacity and extending the institution's mission to include adult students.

In the end, institutional ethos and priorities create a unique balance of centralized and decentralized services and functions. As mentioned by one of our case study authors, mutual appreciation and collaboration are keys to finding each institution's balance.

STEPHEN D. HOLTROP *is dean of graduate and adult programs and professor of education at Huntington University in Huntington, Indiana.*

Index

NEW DIRECTIONS FOR HIGHER EDUCATION

ORDER FORM SUBSCRIPTION AND SINGLE ISSUES

DISCOUNTED BACK ISSUES:

Use this form to receive 20% off all back issues of *New Directions for Higher Education*.
All single issues priced at **$23.20** (normally $29.00)

TITLE	ISSUE NO.	ISBN

Call 888-378-2537 or see mailing instructions below. When calling, mention the promotional code JBNND to receive your discount. For a complete list of issues, please visit www.josseybass.com/go/ndhe

SUBSCRIPTIONS: (1 YEAR, 4 ISSUES)

☐ New Order ☐ Renewal

U.S.	☐ Individual: $89	☐ Institutional: $275
CANADA/MEXICO	☐ Individual: $89	☐ Institutional: $315
ALL OTHERS	☐ Individual: $113	☐ Institutional: $349

Call 888-378-2537 or see mailing and pricing instructions below.
Online subscriptions are available at www.onlinelibrary.wiley.com

ORDER TOTALS:

Issue / Subscription Amount: $ _____

Shipping Amount: $ _____
(for single issues only – subscription prices include shipping)

Total Amount: $ _____

SHIPPING CHARGES:

First Item $6.00
Each Add'l Item $2.00

(No sales tax for U.S. subscriptions. Canadian residents, add GST for subscription orders. Individual rate subscriptions must be paid by personal check or credit card. Individual rate subscriptions may not be resold as library copies.)

BILLING & SHIPPING INFORMATION:

☐ **PAYMENT ENCLOSED:** *(U.S. check or money order only. All payments must be in U.S. dollars.)*

☐ **CREDIT CARD:** ☐VISA ☐MC ☐AMEX

Card number _____Exp. Date_____

Card Holder Name_____Card Issue #_____

Signature _____Day Phone_____

☐ **BILL ME:** *(U.S. institutional orders only. Purchase order required.)*

Purchase order # _____
Federal Tax ID 13559302 • GST 89102-8052

Name_____

Address_____

Phone_____ E-mail_____

Copy or detach page and send to: **John Wiley & Sons, One Montgomery Street, Suite 1200, San Francisco, CA 94104-4594**

Order Form can also be faxed to: **888-481-2665**

PROMO JBNND